Cover photo by Bernhard J. Springer

THE PSYCHIATRIC PATIENT
CASE HISTORIES

Lois Jean Davitz, Ph.D.
Lecturer and Research Associate
Department of Nursing Education
and Institute of Nursing Research
Teachers College, Columbia University

CONSULTANTS IN SELECTION OF CASE MATERIAL AND IDENTIFICATION OF MAJOR CONCEPTS:

P. Herbert Leiderman, Jr., M.D.
Professor of Psychiatry
Stanford University Medical School

Joel R. Davitz, Ph.D.
Professor of Psychology
Director of the Clinical Psychology Program
Teachers College, Columbia University

The Psychiatric Patient

Case Histories

By

Lois Jean Davitz

Consultants

P. Herbert Leiderman, Jr.
Joel R. Davitz

SPRINGER PUBLISHING COMPANY, Inc., NEW YORK

SPRINGER PUBLISHING COMPANY, INC.
200 Park Avenue South
New York, N.Y. 10003

Library of Congress Catalog Card Number: 77-161128
Standard Book Number: 0-8261-1243-9

Designed by Vicki Kessinger

Printed in U.S.A.

For

Michael Andrew

and

Jeffrey Eric

Foreword

Two major issues face workers in the field of mental health services at the present time. The first has to do with how to relate involvement in the community to concern for the individual patient; the second concerns who shall deliver mental health services to individual members of the community. These issues are not new nor are they confined to the mental health field.

Historically, in theology, medicine, and political philosophy, concern for the individual has vied with concern for the group. Since the period of asylums in the eighteenth and nineteenth centuries, psychiatry too has been buffeted by the storms of changing involvements. Much of modern clinical psychiatric theory and practice deals with the individual case; however, the most recent shift in the field – to a group and community approach – might imply a shift away from the individual. That this circumstance should not necessarily follow is amply demonstrated in this volume by Dr. Davitz.

The second major issue – who shall deliver mental health services – also has historical roots. In the past, the soothsayer, shaman, or priest vied with the physician to provide succor and relief for physical and emotional ailments besetting the individual. As our knowledge increased, psychological approaches gradually became institutionalized in guilds of professional mental health workers, psychiatrists, psychiatric nurses, psychologists, and social workers. But beyond these guilds lay the bulk of mental health workers – general duty nurses, technicians, and aides who, by and large, were responsible for providing most of the therapy in both general and specialized psychiatric hospitals. These individuals bore the greatest direct involvement with the individual patient – generally the sickest of the psychiatric patients. The sheer number of cases precluded the possibility of professional mental health workers ever having sufficient time to give individual attention to each patient either in hospitals or in community settings. Thus the issue of who shall deliver these services has already been partially answered – general duty nurses, technicians, and aides will be doing the major share of it. The question that arises is: How shall they deliver these services? It is in this area that Dr. Davitz's book plays the important role of acquainting mental health workers with legitimate clinical problems based on individual cases.

This volume of psychiatric case studies directly addresses itself to both of these major issues. In compiling these fascinating vignettes for clinical teaching, Dr. Davitz has utilized her wide experience in observation, her sensitive eye and ear for the poignant, and her consummate skill in communication. She has refocused attention on the individdual patient, remembering all the while that he is enmeshed in a social and cultural milieu that shapes him and which, in turn, is shaped by him. This concern for the individual is especially critical for the mental health worker who may lack the training and background needed to appreciate this dimension in clinical service professions. Thus the paraprofessional can benefit from the insights and experiences of the professional, and take his rightful place in the ranks of all who are concerned with the alleviation of individual suffering and misery. Hopefully, careful reading of the cases in this volume will have the effect of minimizing the false dichotomies between individual and community, professional and paraprofessional. The magnitude of the task of delivering mental health services is so great that the help and understanding provided by this volume will be welcomed by professionals and paraprofessionals alike.

P. Herbert Leiderman, Jr., M.D.
Stanford, California

Introduction

The relationship between a patient and a psychiatric nurse has undergone significant changes in the last ten years. Prior to this time, patients were sent to psychiatric hospitals isolated from the rest of society. Some stayed until their lonely deaths, completely separated from their former lives. Others, who returned home, frequently bore scars of incriminating diagnostic labels and the past incarcerations that served as reminders of their "shameful" histories.

Nurses working in these institutions were trained in traditional ways. Their attitudes reflected, and indeed reinforced, a system of medical management based upon ostracism or, at best, questionable tolerance.

Because the mentally ill person was viewed as a source of contamination to the community, his isolation was socially justified. Seeing him removed from his environment, sometimes with the assistance of law-enforcing agencies, and then rejected when he attempted to return to society, nurses stressed custodial care. Chronicity was accepted as normal. Nurses attended to numerous administrative chores in the absence of interpersonal activities. They gave deference to their master, the psychiatrist, who usually also functioned as hospital administrator. He was the foremost sanctioned therapeutic agent and, in many instances, the nurse's only mentor.

Thus, nurses were the chief chatelaines in a graduated, rigidly-ordered hierarchy. The jangling ring of oversized keys that were the indispensible parts of their uniforms attested to their limited, proscribed authority. They directed a large corps of menials in the task of "keeping" the patients, an even larger corps. The patients – strange, deserted inhabitants of the fortress – were the lowest ranking group. They frequently attempted to revolt, which justified tighter restrictions on their freedom. Workers were ever vigilant, giving attention to strengthening surveillance.

In 1961, after psychotropic drugs had demonstrated their quieting effect on disturbed patients, the Joint Commission on Mental Illness and Health* issued a report stating that the cure of institutionalization was worse than the disease. The prevailing practice of, and especially the attitudes implicit in, institutionalization were strongly condemned. The use of tranquilizers and the criticism of unproductive confinement constituted the third revolution in psychiatry. In combination, they represented a significant turning point in the care of the mentally ill, as disturbing of previous practices as Pinel's unshackling of asylum inmates and Freud's discovery of the unconscious.

Central to the philosophy of the Commission's report was the belief that a patient is a complex organism, retaining elements of health even while manifesting symptoms of illness. The corollary to this idea was that within a therapeutic milieu all psychiatric workers have potentially therapeutic roles to play in emphasizing inherent positive functions over negative behavior.

As a result of these developments in the last decade, we have seen major alterations in the whole system of psychiatric care, with the focus on *social* and *psychological* rather than *medical* aspects of human behavior. The idea of "patient" has grown to include the person with the presenting problem as inseparable from the human group with whom he interacts. Service to the patient, therefore, can no longer be divorced from attention to significant people about him: his family, friends, neighbors, fellow workers, and indeed the very people who, as psychiatric workers, surround him during and after the period of his emotional crisis. The concept of care has also been expanded. It now includes prevention and rehabilitation as well as remedial assistance, and

* Joint Commission on Mental Illness and Health, *Action For Mental Health*, New York: Basic Books, Inc., 1961.

carries great implications for education.

Changes in housing, showing variation as well as expansion, have followed to meet the patient's newly recognized needs. Agencies have grown up within the community which attempt to eliminate the hospitalized isolation that was so destructive of the patient's humanity. No longer is it necessary for the care agency to be out in the country or on an uninhabited island far from everyone. There are now facilities available for voluntary stays during the day, during the night, or both. Halfway houses make the gradual return to former lives a possible route to health.

Within the hospital itself, doors have been unlocked, except for the most necessary security measures, when the safety of the patient becomes the criterion for restrictions of personal liberty. Visiting hours have been scheduled so that, if a patient cannot go home, someone from his home may come to him. Units within the general hospital have been organized to reduce the stigma of a psychiatric diagnosis by sharing the accommodations of agencies known for serving patients with socially acceptable physical diseases or conditions. Emergency rooms manned around the clock by trained psychiatric staffs are increasingly appearing.

The focus upon the social-psychological aspects of mental illness has brought into prominence a team larger than the traditional duo of physician and nurse. Workers with behavioral science orientations – psychologists, sociologists, social workers – have joined the physician and nurse in assisting the patient to convalescence, a stage that had previously been ignored except for the very few patients who were favored by economic resources and familial support. The role of paraprofessional workers has been reevaluated, and their potential for assisting the patient to reenter the community has been recognized.

Communication has been identified as of central importance in delivering mental health services. Channels for interaction among mental health workers, patients, and community members are being widened so that the person who is ill may receive therapy, the person who has been ill may be assisted with rehabilitation, and the person who has been exposed to illness may be taught to avoid it and to seek resources which encourage social-psychological growth. This mobile process implies that the hospital is but one arena for therapeutic action. Workers are now moving out, from one milieu to another, following the patient as he progresses in his ability to function in his familiar environment to the best of his capacity.

And the central figure who accompanies the patient along this complex road map is the nurse. She, too, has been set free. Although she shares some of each of the attributes of the members of the mental health team, she has qualifications that are hers alone. The nurse and the physician share an educational background that is based on the medical model. Including biology, anatomy, and physiology, this knowledge supplements the behavioral sciences in their curricula. Considering the delicate equilibrium of emotional and physical factors in health and illness, this foundation provides the nurse with a basis for viewing the patient in his totality.

Like the practicing physician and social worker, the nurse has entrée into the patient's familiar surroundings. She is able to visit in the patient's home and is respected by the public for her service there. It has been amply documented that the visiting nurse moves freely and without danger in neighborhoods where most strangers may be unwelcome and viewed with distrust. In the community, the nurse, of all health workers, is trusted and welcomed.

The nurse is similar to the group worker in that traditionally she has been exposed to people in the aggregate. As a member of the largest department of workers within an agency she is usually responsible for numbers of patients, shares information and tasks with a large staff of nursing personnel, and works closely with members of other departments and with specialists in every field. She is familiar with representatives from the community: the patient's visitors, policemen, welfare workers, clergymen.

But unlike these specialists, she has two other characteristics which are unique. One of these is her presence at all times, night and day, during the patient's hospital stay. The physician, the psychologist, the social worker, the activity therapist, and numerous other workers may carry out their services for circumscribed times. But when they leave, the nurse remains. Many mental health facilities do not even employ such specialists. Then these other roles are assumed by the nurse because there is always the nursing staff.

It is the nurse's "thereness" that constitutes her other unique characteristic. Of all the mental health workers she has not only the longest contact with the patient, but also the most intimate. She meets the patient's most elementary physiological needs: his need for shelter, for food, for rest, for cleanliness. She meets the patient's most necessary emotional needs: his need for protection, for socialization, for recognition. She is familiar with all aspects of the patient's day. She sees him when he gets up in the morning and when he goes to bed at night. She knows him at his moments of deepest vulnerability and she is there when he seeks help most abjectly. She knows how he reacts to the loneliness of an unfamiliar and frightening situation; which of his visitors cause him to react; how he responds to the individual members of the hospital community. The nurse sees manifestations of the patient's behavior that many other workers may never see or be called upon directly to support. It is in these moments of crisis that learning may take place — and the nurse is there.

The effectiveness of the nurse in her newly expanded role will depend in part on her understanding of the dynamics involved in interpersonal interactions. Thus, the practice involved in reading and analyzing case histories is an important technique for learning to apply psychological principles and psychiatric concepts to actual situations.

FANNY SIEGEL, R.N., B.S., ED.M.
Director of Continuing Education,
Program for Psychiatric Nurses,
Teachers College, Columbia University

Contents

You turn your face, but does it bring your heart?

from *Andrea Del Sarto*
by Robert Browning

1

Nothing To Worry About

Concerned about Miss Hansen's failure to answer his repeated calls, the superintendent of her rooming house notified a police emergency squad. The door was forced open, and Miss Hansen was discovered lying in bed, weak, emaciated, semiconscious. Aware that help had arrived, she murmured, "I'm so grateful someone came."

While she was being lifted to a stretcher, she whispered apologies for the disturbance she was causing. "I always was
the one who took care of everything. Momma said she (1)
wouldn't have known what to do without me. I tried to call. I tried so hard. No one heard through the door."

The superintendent told a police officer that Miss Hansen lived alone, had no relatives, and was a good, kind old lady who apparently managed on a meager income. "She was some kind of retired teacher. I cashed her Social Security checks." He was certain she was not on welfare, but he did

1. With increasing age there is, of course, a change in physical capabilities and capacity for self-care. Sometimes there is a lag in the change of a person's self-concept, and problems may develop as a result of the incongruity between a person's physical state and his view of himself.

not know much else about her. "My wife knows more. She gets around and talks to the roomers. I can ask her. She'll come up and pack the old woman's things. It looks like a last trip for her."

Miss Hansen was admitted to a medical unit at the City Hospital and treated for shock and malnutrition. Within a few days she responded to treatment and was able to converse freely with the staff.

"You snapped back beautifully," said Miss Pedersen, a floor nurse. "We should have you trotting around here in no time."

"For an old lady, I did recover rather quickly," replied Miss Hansen.

"Oh, come now. You're not so old."

"I bet you couldn't possibly guess my age," teased Miss Hansen.

"I'd say you're about sixty-five."

"Eighty-three, soon eighty-four," replied Miss Hansen. She smiled and drew her forefinger across her teeth. "They're all mine. Not one cavity. The young doctor this morning couldn't believe me when I showed him. He said he had never had a patient my age with her own teeth! He told me I was medical history! He confessed that he had six false teeth, and he's only thirty-three. Oh, dear," she added worriedly, "I don't know whether I should have told his secret. You musn't tell him what I've said. But then I didn't really tell you which doctor it was, did I?"

Frail and diminutive, Miss Hansen had the appearance of a much younger woman. Her pink skin was unlined except for a few slivers of wrinkles near her eyes and at the corners of her mouth. Her eyes were clear, with only a trace of filigreed red veins in the whites. She told the nurses that she had only started wearing glasses for reading after turning seventy.

"You've bounced back like a rubber ball," Miss Pedersen repeatedly told Miss Hansen.

"It's been a good life for me," said Miss Hansen.

Miss Hansen had taught kindergarten for forty-three years in a school within walking distance of her home. She told the staff that when she had first lived in the neighborhood, there were trees and wide, empty fields. Over the years she had watched the neighborhood change. Each day, it seemed to her, as she walked the six blocks to the school, the area looked different. New buildings replaced old; empty lots were swallowed up by large housing developments.

Miss Hansen lived with her parents. Her father died when she was fifty, and she and her mother moved into a small flat in the same area. "Momma worked until she was seventy-four as a sales clerk. I think it was walking that kept us young. We never rode anywhere. Walking is good for you," she told Miss Pedersen.

"Don't worry, we get plenty of that around here," answered Miss Pedersen. "Sitting is more my style," she said playfully.

"Oh, heavens no," insisted Miss Hansen. "Momma and I walked and walked every evening until the neighborhood changed. It's not safe to walk any more. But we got up early every day and walked, and on weekends Momma and I (2)
were up walking. We were members of a bird-watching club that met on Sundays in the park."

"Your mother?" asked Miss Pedersen. "Does she still live with you?"

"Momma died twenty years ago," said Miss Hansen.

After three weeks of rest and treatment, Miss Hansen

2. Among elderly patients, earlier memories may seem more vivid and significant than recent events. In addition to possible physiological reasons for this, the strong emotional meaning of these earlier experiences may account for their significance to the patient. In the present case, Miss Hansen's relationship to her mother was probably a central part of her life for many years, and even after twenty years this relationship obviously retains its significance for her.

seemed to be completely recovered and was scheduled for discharge. Concerned about her living alone, Miss Pedersen questioned the advisability of sending her out of the hospital without supervision. She expressed her feelings to the chief resident in charge of Miss Hansen's case and to the nursing supervisor, Mrs. Axel.

"We can't keep her here forever," said Mrs. Axel. "She is a relatively healthy woman."

"We're a hospital, not a nursing home," said the resident.

"I don't think she can manage alone. She rambles sometimes about her Momma. Then I discovered that Momma has been dead for twenty years."

"What do you want us to do?" asked the resident. "We need the bed space. She's as healthy as she'll ever be – remarkably so, I'd say, considering her age."

Mrs. Axel agreed. "She isn't on welfare. She has independent means. She gets a pension and Social Security. We can't tell her how she is to run her life. It's another thing if *she* asks for help. But right now she has to make her own decisions. If I were her age, I don't think I would want someone coming in to me and telling me I'm an old lady and I better not live alone. See this from her point of view," she told Miss Pedersen.

The following morning Miss Pedersen discussed the subject with Miss Hansen.

"You must be happy now that you're ready to go home!"

"What do you mean?" asked Miss Hansen.

"You're all better. The doctor said you could leave any time now."

"The way a place changes so," said Miss Hansen. "Daddy bought a house in that area because it was country. He would have been miserable if he had lived to see what happened. I told Momma that it is a blessing he is gone. I used to play in a field where there is a twenty-five story building. Imagine that! Momma and I sold the house. We should have kept it, Momma said, and waited for a better price, but it was after Daddy went and there was no point in two old ladies keeping a place. Besides, Momma and I didn't need that much room. I hated to leave the neighborhood because it was so close to my school. Did I tell you that I taught kindergarten for forty-three years? My, that does seem long but it isn't at all when you live through the years. The time passed very quickly. Maybe it did seem slow after Christmas, but then we had spring coming on. The winters were hard because the little ones can't do their boots and scarves, and they come bundled so. We lost so many things. I wish you could have seen our Lost and Found (3) at the school office. We had enough snow caps and mittens to dress an army!"

"The staff will miss you, Miss Hansen. We'd be lucky if all our patients were as good as you've been. You've been a delightfully easy patient, I must say. If you stayed any longer we couldn't ever let you go."

"Leaving?" asked Miss Hansen. "Leaving is painful. That's how Momma and I felt when we moved from a house into a tiny flat. It wasn't all that small, but after the space of our house it seemed dismal. Momma cried, but I couldn't let on how I felt. It wouldn't do to have both of us feeling blue at the same time. I kept the flat till after Momma left and then only about five years ago I moved into a rooming house. Was it five years ago? I don't recall exactly."

"You're all better. You've made a great recovery, snapped right back. The doctor said you could go home any time now."

"The one with the bad teeth? He's a lovely young man. He should watch his teeth. We always had a dentist come

3. Leaving the hospital is probably experienced by the patient as threatening, and she psychologically escapes from the threat by going off on an apparent tangent. The nurse evidently doesn't recognize the threat to the patient and continues the conversation as if the patient had heard and happily accepted the announcement of her recovery.

to school to check the children's teeth. Parents could be so careless. Even the very little ones would sometimes have awful teeth. Yes, he's a lovely young man. He came to see me this morning."

"Do you remember what he said?"

"He told me that when he was my age he hoped that he would have my energy, health, and sound mind."

"Is that all?"

"Should he have said something else? He told me to take vitamins every day and a drop of wine to help me sleep. I could never do that. Daddy would be horrified."

"Yes, but did he also talk to you about your diet? We do want to talk about your diet before you go. You haven't been eating properly. We can talk about what you should eat every day. I'll give you a list of foods for breakfast, lunch. . . ."

"Won't there be lunch today?" interrupted Miss Hansen.

"Certainly. I mean foods you should have when you leave."

"Leave?" Miss Hansen appeared confused. "I hadn't expected to leave. I was just getting settled. Moving is so hard. When Momma and I gave up the house it was so difficult getting rid of everything. We had a lovely old couch that Momma had since Daddy and she got married and it was too big to go up the steps to the apartment. How Momma cried, and she had me crying. It wasn't that the couch was all that valuable except to Momma and me, but the idea of having to throw it away was terrible."

Miss Hansen continued to discuss Momma's reactions to this first move and her feelings when she moved a second time, ". . . which Momma didn't know about. Momma is dead, isn't she? Gone now – twenty years."

That night Miss Hansen remained awake, whimpering and crying for "Momma." Sedation had no effect. She soiled her bed repeatedly. The next morning she refused to get up, insisting that she was feeling unwell. In response to the nurses' efforts to reassure her, Miss Hansen continuously cried for "Momma," her hands caressing a silver crucifix tied on a frayed black ribbon around her neck.

Miss Pedersen requested that a staff psychiatrist see Miss Hansen immediately. Upon his recommendation, she was moved to a small psychiatric unit where she remained under observation. Throughout the nights and days of the following week her behavior remained unchanged. She (4)
alternately wept and called for "Momma," and she lost control of both urinary and bowel functions. The attending psychiatrist arranged to have her transferred to a state psychiatric hospital where she was assigned to a general female ward.

* * *

The patients in the psychiatric hospital slept in large dormitory rooms with beds arranged in rows. Each was assigned a small dresser for personal items. The patients ranged in age from sixteen to eighty-five, with the majority between the ages of forty and sixty. There was a frequent turnover of patients, since relatively few remained in residence more than two years. Those patients who were not considered capable of returning to their homes were routinely assigned to nursing homes or to outlying state hospitals with larger facilities.

* * *

Miss Hansen was placed on tranquilizers. The first few days she did not respond; the dosage was increased substantially. After four days, her outburst of tears and pleas for "Momma" subsided. On the fifth day following admis-

4. With the threat of being forced to leave the hospital and the accompanying fear and anxiety, Miss Hansen regresses, loses self-control, and becomes ill. It is unlikely that these are signs of malingering, but rather that they reflect the intensity of the threat she experiences.

sion, she awakened and cheerfully greeted other patients in the room. She introduced herself.

"I'm Miss Hansen. It's like the first day at school. I feel like a new pupil. 'Good morning,' I would say. 'Good morning,' answered the children. I taught kindergarten for forty-three years. Retired now. I do miss the children."

The other patients nodded. Several repeated their names.

"It won't take me long to learn everybody's name. Perhaps there is a list. I could make a list and then we could all have a copy."

Miss Lowens, a staff nurse, came in to check on Miss Hansen.

"We want to get you settled."

"I'm fine," replied Miss Hansen. "I fit in quite easily."

"Would you like to unpack your suitcase? Each of you has a dresser. This is yours." Miss Lowens showed her the dresser. She also explained that Miss Hansen would quickly learn the routine. There were schedules to follow and meal times came promptly at assigned hours. "We'll have another patient show you around."

"Oh, I am sure I'll be fine. Did anyone see my scarf? I always like my scarf around my neck because of drafts. So many children come to school without any scarves. It's so important on cold days."

"We might check your suitcase," replied Miss Lowens.

The suitcase was pulled out from beneath the bed, and Miss Hansen opened it. "The scarf is missing," she cried. "It was Momma's best scarf."

"I am sure it's here," Miss Lowens reassured her.

"Someone took it," insisted Miss Hansen. "We began to have this trouble in school when the neighborhood went down. At first, it was only a pencil and eraser. That's how it started, but soon I couldn't even leave my handbag on my desk. I had to lock it in a drawer! Little ones I had, little five year olds! Hands clean, faces clean, but they began stealing."

The other patients gathered around Miss Lowens while

she searched the suitcase for the missing scarf. As she lifted up a number of articles, several patients lunged forward and snatched them from Miss Lowens' hands.

"My slippers!" shouted one woman.

"My handkerchief," screamed a second patient. "She's a thief. I knew we shouldn't have left her in the room. She kept watching till we went out, then she stole."

Miss Hansen became upset and apologized. "I thought they were mine," she insisted. "I had a pair of slippers just like these. Momma gave them to me for my birthday. The handkerchief, isn't that an *M* on the handkerchief? A little girl gave it to me as a Christmas present."

"It's a *T*," said Miss Lowens.

"A *T*? I thought it was an *M*. You must have your handkerchief back, my dear," Miss Hansen said, giving it to the patient who claimed that it was hers.

She looked around the room. "So many beds," she whispered. "I always had my own room. And the big wardrobe. Didn't they bring my big wardrobe that Daddy used?"

"This is your dresser, Miss Hansen."

"This is all I have – one dresser? I can manage. I can manage very well. You would be surprised what treasures my desk could hold. Kindergarten teachers always had the smallest desks. That wasn't always fair, you know."

"You're due for a hairwash," said Mrs. Tomas, an attendant, coming into the room with a clipboard. "She hasn't been washed since she came. How is she today? You ready to get your hair washed? My, you got a lot of hair," said Mrs. Tomas. "Like a little girl. Thick isn't it? You're going to take all morning. Come along now."

"My hair washed?" Miss Hansen appeared surprised. "I always do my own hair. I had to do Momma's, but then it was the arthritis in her joints. Her hands were all buckled over, and she couldn't unbend them. It made her so sad to think I had to wash and comb her hair for her. I washed it with egg. Her hair is so white and the eggs made it glisten – snow hair is what the children called it. Momma came to school to visit my classes."

"Eggs?" said Mrs. Tomas. "For hair? Honey, you don't come from where I do, that's for sure. Where I comes from we eats our eggs! We don't wash hair in eggs. We got good shampoo here. It's good for nits and lice." She turned to Miss Lowens. "You know, we'll have to get some turpentine. That new patient I had this morning had a headful of nits. You haven't got nits, I can see that," Mrs. Tomas told Miss Hansen.

"Heavens no," said Miss Hansen. "I had them once," she confided. "A little girl, the sweetest child came to class. I thought I saw something strange in her head. Then, before
5 lunch one little boy who sat near her wasn't paying any attention to me. I walked back and he was popping nits! Nits! I had to send her home with a note. Momma was shocked to find some in my hair."

After Miss Hansen left with Mrs. Tomas to have her hair washed, the other patients crowded around Miss Lowens with their complaints about Miss Hansen's stealing. They were angry and upset. None of the dressers could be locked; the door of the room was always open. They insisted a guard be placed around Miss Hansen to prevent a recurrence of the stealing.

Miss Lowens tried to calm them, explaining that Miss Hansen was a new patient and had been very confused since her arrival. It was evident that she felt much better. She certainly wasn't the kind of person who would deliberately steal. "She was a teacher. Now we must give her a chance."

"Teachers are people," argued one patient. "What makes you think they're so honest?"

5. Once again, the past seems much more meaningful to the patient than the present, and if one considers the contrast in the emotional meanings of her past and present situations, it is not difficult to empathize with Miss Hansen.

"I didn't mean that," said Miss Lowens, "but she really seems to be very nice and we must wait and give her a chance to be herself."

"And then what?" asked one patient.

"I can assure you," said Miss Lowens, "that we will do something about the matter."

Several other patients who had adjoining beds said they couldn't tolerate the smell. "She 'makes' in her bed. She should be in diapers."

This matter, too, was being considered, Miss Lowens said, and the staff would decide what was best to do about it.

The patients left the room disgruntled, complaining of their dissatisfaction with Miss Lowens' responses to their problems. One said that was typical of the staff. "As long as they're not bothered and you keep minding your own business, they're happy. They don't do anything for the patients around here."

Later, Miss Lowens talked about Miss Hansen to Mrs. Deil, who had been the nursing supervisor on the floor for ten years. She said that the other patients were annoyed. They felt that their belongings weren't safe. The odors from Miss Hansen's bed also disturbed them and several insisted that she be removed from the room or placed in diapers. "I was told, 'If she's a baby, treat her like one.'"

Mrs. Deil hesitated to act immediately. Miss Hansen appeared to be a gentle woman who might only be confused by her new surroundings. Her explanation that she thought the articles belonged to her seemed reasonable. The slippers had been taken from the woman whose bed was next to hers. The slippers might very well have been on Miss Hansen's side of the aisle, and she could easily have assumed they belonged to her. The other articles were of little value and were clearly the kind of personal items Miss Hansen could have had: a handkerchief, a sachet, a small package of tissues, and a comb. Mrs. Deil suggested that they wait a few days, observe Miss Hansen, and periodically check her dresser and suitcase.

The wetting at night presented another problem. Miss Hansen had been upset at the move to the hospital. She had been under medication, and this might have caused her to lose night control. She was being taken off the heavy dosage, and Mrs. Deil thought it best to wait and see how she reacted. She also suggested that Miss Hansen not be given any liquids after dinner, and that the attendants be told to take her to the toilet before going to bed.

Mrs. Deil said she was going to talk to Miss Hansen that afternoon to obtain a full case history and would have other suggestions regarding handling her after the interview.

At two in the afternoon, Miss Hansen was asked into Mrs. Deil's office. Immediately after the door closed, Miss Hansen emptied the contents of her handbag on Mrs. Deil's desk.

"I would like you to keep these in a safe place." She handed Mrs. Deil a bankbook, several blank checks, Social Security card, pension identification, and a large brown envelope. "My birth certificate, Daddy's, Momma's, and cemetery papers for all of us are in there. I can't trust the other patients. I shouldn't say anything, I suppose, but there
6 was trouble today. I'd feel so much better if I knew you were keeping these things safely locked up for me." Mrs. Deil talked informally with Miss Hansen about her feelings regarding the hospital. She told her they were happy to have her and certainly felt that Miss Hansen would do well.

Miss Hansen replied that she didn't understand why she
7 had been sent to the hospital. She missed her own place where she knew the people, knew the neighborhood, and had her own possessions.

6. Expressing her distrust of other patients may reflect Miss Hansen's projection of her own unacceptable impulses. In effect, she is saying, "I don't steal; others want to steal from me."

7. Despite her real and probably justified fears of being

"I know I don't have much any more. But I gave up the apartment after Momma left, and there was no sense in keeping everything. The new room was small. I wanted to save money, too. I knew I was getting on in years. It's one thing Momma always worried about, having money when she was older. She told me never to spend too much, not that she minded what I did with my money, but she said. 'One day you'll find yourself old and without money. It's a terrible thing to happen to anyone.'"

"But you have money."

"Oh yes, enough to live on. I get my pension and Social Security. The pension isn't too much. I started teaching so long ago. We didn't have benefits like they do now. And then so much of my savings went for illness, Daddy's funeral, and Momma's. Momma wanted a new denture just before she died. That costs so much. I had it made just like she wanted. Four hundred dollars." Miss Hansen reached down in her handbag, took out a small bag, and unzipped it. She held up the denture to show Mrs. Deil.

"Do you have any relatives we might contact, Miss Hansen?"

"Children? I was never married. I had thousands of children if I ever counted them up. They were only mine for a year, sometimes two, if we held them back. These children are all grown up now. I've had them come back and see me. I remember one little boy who couldn't tie his shoes and was such a devil. One day he pushed open the door of my room; the children were all listening to a story I was reading and he just came in. I didn't know him at all. He was so grown up. He had to remind me that he was once a wild little creature in my class. I could have cried. I never did forget his coming back like that to see me. And he had so

unable to live on her own, the patient also needs to maintain her sense of self-respect as a person who can take care of herself.

many other teachers but remembered his kindergarten teacher best of all."

"Is there anyone at all we might call, Miss Hansen?"

"There was just Daddy, Momma, and me; then there was Momma and me; and then me alone. It's like musical chairs. Do you know that in forty-three years, the one game the children loved so was musical chairs? Do you play it here? Now what in the world made me think of that now? I haven't thought of musical chairs since I was teaching."

"You were thinking about the name of a friend."

"Was I?"

"Someone we might call?"

"I don't know if he is feeling well himself."

"Do you have his name?"

"Mr. Alfred Locke."

"His address?"

"I have it written down somewhere," said Miss Hansen. "We taught in the same school. He was in charge of the school orchestra. When I first started teaching, we even had an orchestra for kindergarten! It was amazing what Mr. Locke did. Then the children started changing. They weren't the same. Old families moved away. The new ones coming in never thought much about the music program. All the instruments got bad, and we couldn't afford new ones. It made Mr. Locke so unhappy, but like me, he just stayed it out. You build up seniority in a school and hate to start over. It's not easy. Then we got to the point where we waited to retire. The year before he retired, vandals came into the school and broke all the instruments, every single one smashed. That day stands out so in my mind. There wasn't any orchestra that whole last year. Mr. Locke came down to the kindergarten room and just sat. Momma thought the world of him. Momma." Miss Hansen stood up. "May I go to the bathroom please? 'You've gone once this morning' is what I would say." Miss Hansen felt her wet dress and stockings and looked up tearfully at Mrs. Deil. "I'm too late."

"We'll get you cleaned up," said Mrs. Deil. "Come on now. That's a good girl."

"You won't tell Momma?" asked Miss Hansen.

"No."

"Just our secret," said Miss Hansen.

Late that afternoon Miss Hansen complained of feeling dizzy. Her hands gestured vaguely. She said that her head was splitting but cried when Miss Lowens tried to give her aspirin. She lay down in bed whimpering about her legs feeling stiff, her heart ready "to explode." When the patients lined up for supper, Miss Hansen refused to join them. She insisted that she was much too weak and remained in bed. An aide brought a tray to her bedside and fed Miss Hansen. Her throat felt tight, she said, and swallowing was difficult. Food dribbled out of the corners of her mouth. The aide wiped her mouth and found a clean hospital gown. Miss Lowens gave her a sleeping pill and Miss Hansen rested quietly the rest of the night. The next morning she rose, 8
quickly made her bed and surprised the staff by being first on the breakfast line.

* * *

Miss Hansen's case was considered at the regular biweekly staff conference for nurses, attendants, aides, social worker, and psychologists. Dr. Torrey, staff psychiatrist, chaired the meeting.

Miss Hansen's lapses of control over body functions were discussed first. One of the attendants reported that "She goes off and on. Sometimes she's dry as a bone. Stays that way

8. It is possible, of course, that this incident may be a consequence of some physical illness or disability, but it is also possible that its basis was primarily psychological. That is, Miss Hansen's physical illness would "explain" the loss of urinary control and thus provide a rationalization to maintain her sense of self-respect.

for three nights running; the next night she floods the bed. The other patients sure do let you know quick enough. Why does she do that?" she asked Dr. Torrey. "She seems so reasonable. I've talked with her and she makes good sense."

"This happens," answered Dr. Torrey. "Lots of factors are involved. Her age and any stresses contribute to the condition."

"She's got nothing worrying her here," said Mrs. Tomas. "It's like a hotel, I told her. Food on time, bedding all clean; hot and cold water. I told her to stop seeing it as a hospital. It's a hotel."

"From your point of view she is comfortable and secure. But she has been independent and might resent the routines here. I think we might encourage her participation in some activities. She needs some stimulation. Having her just walk around all day isn't wise. She's capable of much more involvement in activities. How does she relate to the other patients?"

"If you ask me," answered Miss Frane, "I wonder why she's here in the first place. She's got ups and downs, but who doesn't. She does very well with the other patients. I've seen her go up to Tibbey and fix her shawl and I've watched her go over to Miss Zemar and comb her hair. She even tied a ribbon in it and told Zemar that she looked pretty. She acts sometimes like a momma with them. She's always fussing over the patients. I heard her remind some about time to get their pills. She got all upset when the medication line wasn't straight. She told them they had to stand in line, and I was surprised myself, but they listened to her and they got into a line and she stood there watching to see someone didn't shove. She doesn't seem off the deep end to me."

Dr. Torrey agreed that Miss Hansen did indeed have long periods of lucidity. He knew that she appeared coherent and in touch, but " . . . there are also times when she is confused and disoriented. It is at such times that she regresses. Just because she can function here in the hospital doesn't mean that she can function outside."

"I'm not so sure," said Miss Lowens. "She wants so much to talk to people about Momma. Here we listen, but how much can we listen to the same stories? She goes over and over the neighborhood, the way the area changed, her school, the children, and Momma's death. That's all she has left from eighty-three years. She sometimes talks as if her mother were still alive. I've listened to her and she switches back and forth."

"That will happen," reflected Dr. Torrey.

"What do we do when she goes on and on like that? I find myself tuning her out," said Miss Frane. "The first time I listened and the second, but as Miss Lowens said, it's the third and fourth time about how Momma wouldn't like it, or about how the couch was too big to go up the stairs that I tune her out."

Dr. Torrey talked about Miss Hansen's need for listeners. "I don't think you should worry about reacting or responding to what she says all the time. She just wants to be sure you are listening."

"You got it easy," said Miss Frane. "Once a week, but I had to sit with her and hold her hand and she kept calling (9)
me 'Momma' last night. When that happens I get feeling funny. She also keeps talking about some man named Locke."

Mrs. Deil said that she had spoken with Miss Hansen and had Mr. Locke's address and phone number. She was planning to contact him and suggest that he come to visit Miss Hansen.

Dr. Torrey felt this certainly would be a good idea. Mr. Locke was someone from Miss Hansen's past life who shared

9. There is indeed a significant difference between seeing a patient for an hour once a week and listening to the same patient day in and day out. Sometimes advice based on brief contact with a patient fails to take into account the somewhat different demands made in daily interactions.

her interests and who would be receptive to stories about events and people they both knew. Dr. Torrey also suggested that the staff make an effort to involve Miss Hansen in some of the patient activities. "We can't expect too much, but she should feel a part of the group." He cautioned them against giving her too much responsibility but advised them to try to engage her in tasks that would be meaningful both to herself and to the unit.

* * *

Encouraged by Miss Lowens, the patient committee that supervised the linen closet asked Miss Hansen to help them. She enthusiastically accepted the offer. "I've been so idle. This will take the time off my hands." After a week, the patients complained to Miss Lowens that Miss Hansen "had messed everything up."

The patients were supposed to sort the sheets, towels, and pillowcases when they arrived from the central laundry. The first task was to count them to make certain the order had been correctly filled. Miss Hansen was asked to count the pillowcases. "She took all morning and said we was short. I complained to Linen Supply downstairs. They sent someone up. We counted and we was two over. She said she was a teacher. I never knew a teacher couldn't count."

They made another attempt to have her help. She was asked to hand out towels and to collect soiled towels from each patient. "She started off fine. Then we finds clean towels
(10) with dirty towels. We can't have this," insisted the patient in charge. "I'm responsible for linen."

Miss Lowens explained to Miss Hansen that she might want to help on another assignment because the committee

10. Involving elderly patients in activities is certainly a desirable goal in most cases, but one must also consider the possible frustrations and problems likely to be encountered. Thus, care must be taken to match the activity with the patient's current capacities.

on linen already had three people.

"Did I do something wrong?" asked Miss Hansen. "I wondered. The other women were so quiet. They didn't want to talk to me. They blamed me for the pillowcases, but when I counted we were short. Someone put them back when I wasn't looking. They put back extras. Did they tell you? We had two more than we were supposed to have."

Miss Hansen was assigned to help with sweeping and emptying ashtrays. She willingly agreed. "I don't smoke myself. I never did. Daddy loved his cigars. Momma always takes out the ashtrays before Daddy comes home. It's so funny how all day there isn't an ashtray in the house, and at six, ashtrays appear. One night Momma had a headache. Daddy said he knew something was wrong because there wasn't an ashtray out like usual. I do think little chores are so important. I always had my lists of children posted. Why, I think we could do the same here. Gold stars each day. Do you think the patients would enjoy having their names up with gold stars?"

Every effort to involve Miss Hansen in some aspect of patient activities met with failure. She would respond eagerly, but her interest waned after each initial, sporadic attempt.

Miss Lowens felt discouraged and reported her feelings to Mrs. Deil. Miss Lowens had completed her nurse's training in an associate degree program. Currently she was taking courses toward a baccalaureate degree. In addition to this academic training, she had represented the hospital nursing staff at continuing education workshops designed to sensitize psychiatric nurses to patient interaction and group leadership.

Miss Lowens was disappointed that she seemed unable to work constructively with Miss Hansen. "We're just maintaining her – if that," she said. "I cannot seem to relate to her. She's losing ground rather than gaining. When I first decided to work in psychiatry, I saw myself in a therapeutic role. With Miss Hansen I am nothing more than the keeper

11 of a body. I certainly don't see how I am helping her. There is something missing and I haven't any idea what to do."

Mrs. Deil felt that Miss Lowens was projecting her own feelings onto Miss Hansen. "You feel that it is important for her to be occupied. She might prefer at her age to be an observer – to remain uninvolved. With this kind of elderly patient, sometimes the best thing we can do is to see that they have food and are warm and clean."

"Is that enough?" asked Miss Lowens. She asked Mrs. Deil if she had contacted Miss Hansen's friend. "I think it would be meaningful if she had some visitors. It must be lonely for her with no one from her own life to talk to."

Miss Lowens volunteered to take on the task and Mrs. Deil gave her the slip of paper with Mr. Locke's phone number and address. Miss Lowens spent the afternoon on the telephone. After a series of calls, she reached the retired superintendent of the building, having traced his name through the realty agency who managed the apartment house. She was told that Mr. Alfred Locke was dead. The man who answered her questions said that he wasn't quite sure how long exactly, but he knew it must be every bit of ten or twelve years.

* * *

"Miss Hansen," said Miss Lowens, "didn't I give you some garters the other day?"

11. The definition of success and failure in any particular case depends, in part, on one's expectations. This may be a special problem in working with geriatric cases, when expectations appropriate for younger patients are often simply inappropriate. Very significant service can be provided for the elderly patient, and one can gain a real sense of professional satisfaction in providing these services. But this requires an empathic understanding of the patient's needs and his psychological as well as physical capacities.

"Garters?"

"Yes, long elastic garters. I gave them to you. You're going to trip over your stockings. Do you remember where you put them?"

"Garters?" Miss Hansen held out her hand. The garters were wrapped around her wrist as bracelets.

"I'll help you put them on," said Miss Lowens. "Now we'll go back to the room and get your dress on right. It's inside out. Come on now." She took Miss Hansen by the hand and led her back to the room. "We'll get you fixed up." We'll get your dress on right, your stockings pulled up and then we're going to find your shoes. You have on one shoe and one sneaker. Are they under the bed?"

"No," said Miss Hansen.

"They aren't here," said Miss Lowens, stooping down and searching under the bed.

She checked the top of the bed. "Your shoe is under your blanket. Why?"

"I didn't want to lose it," explained Miss Hansen.

"Now we'll get you ready."

"Like a party," said Miss Hansen. "The children came so beautifully dressed for a party. Momma said I always looked that way when I went to a party. Am I going somewhere?"

"No."

"Then why fuss? It's kind of you to bother about an old lady whose time is running out," said Miss Hansen. "I remember doing this for Momma. She always was so careful about her appearance. She would never be out on Sunday without her hat. Then toward the end I did everything the way you have to do it now. I feel like I would like to rest awhile. I don't sleep well," said Miss Hansen.

"Have you had trouble sleeping? You should have told someone."

"It's not that bad. Only at night," said Miss Hansen, "and then I remember what Momma said just near the end. She said it was getting dark and why did I pull down the shades. I was alone with her and it was a bright sunny day. I knew something was going wrong with Momma. She said it was getting darker and darker. Do you think she knew what was happening?"

"I don't know."

"I wanted to ask. I am so sorry I didn't ask. She might have told me. It's not a question to ask but I would have wanted to know if Momma still believed."

"Believed what, Miss Hansen?"

"There was another place."

"We must have faith."

"Faith?" asked Miss Hansen. "I wonder. I get frightened now. An old lady. I sometimes wonder what I'm doing around so long. I'm no good."

"You're very good, Miss Hansen. You'll be up and around as quick as a wink. We'll have to get you a shower. You're drenched. Now we want to plan, Miss Hansen. There are
(12) many interesting things to do around here. You have to get hold of yourself."

"That's what I told Momma after Daddy went. Get hold of yourself. Oh, she fell apart but she did get hold of herself."

"That's what you're going to do. You have lots of people here. Miss Hansen, is there some other friend you have?"

"Mrs. Deil keeps asking me the same question. I gave her

12. Concern about death and dying is a common and perfectly normal focus of attention for geriatric patients, and others often fail to respond to this concern because of their own unresolved problems in this area. In this case, the nurse rejects the patient's obvious concern about death, trying to avoid the topic with bland statements about faith or the need for a shower. This kind of avoidance can hardly be helpful to the patient, and in fact may be quite disturbing. In working with such patients, therefore, it is most important to resolve one's own problems about death and to develop the capacity to discuss the patient's concerns honestly and without anxiety.

the name of Mr. Locke. Did she call him?"

"We couldn't reach him," responded Miss Lowens.

"Oh, I knew you couldn't," said Miss Hansen. "He's dead, isn't he? I read his name long ago in the obituary pages. They're all gone from the staff at the school. Every single one but me. I only gave her the name because she kept asking me for a friend's name, and I worried so she would think it odd that I didn't have someone to call."

"Now let's get your hair combed."

"I get to worrying sometimes."

"You mustn't worry, Miss Hansen. There's nothing to worry about here. You're safe here."

"It's an awful thing to say," said Miss Hansen. "But when Momma was going, I kept praying so hard that I would go first. It didn't work out that way. If it did, what would have happened to Momma? But that's how I felt."

"Now you must put those thoughts out of your head. There's so much to enjoy in life," said Miss Lowens. "We're going to give you a nice warm bath. We'll get you all cleaned up and dry. We'll just wear some heavy panties so you won't worry about messing yourself."

"If Momma went first, then it meant that I *had* to be last. I didn't want to be the last to go – alone."

Miss Hansen whimpered for "Momma."

"A nice warm bath," Miss Lowens repeated. "Then let's think of something you could really enjoy doing this afternoon."

NOTHING TO WORRY ABOUT

1. The kind of humorous responses Miss Pedersen makes in her first encounter with Miss Hansen are frequently used by staff members to establish rapport and to reduce a patient's tension. What is your evaluation of this technique? Do you feel older patients react favorably to playful verbal

exchanges? What are your opinions about the use of humor in developing a relationship with a patient?

2. Because of Miss Hansen's advanced age, Miss Pedersen questions her ability to live independently. Discuss some of the cues in Miss Hansen's behavior which prompted Miss Pedersen to make this assessment.

3. Mrs. Axel and the resident feel that Miss Hansen does not belong in a hospital. Mrs. Axel further comments that this patient must make her own decision about living arrangements. Under what circumstances would you disagree? Under what conditions might you agree with this point of view?

4. Miss Pedersen recommends that Miss Hansen be seen by a psychiatrist. On what basis did she make this suggestion? Do you agree with her judgment of the situation?

5. On the psychiatric ward, Miss Lowens assists Miss Hansen to orient herself to the unfamiliar surroundings. She says, "Another patient will show you around." What might be the reasons for involving other patients in the care and guidance of a newly admitted patient?

6. Miss Hansen's conversation regarding her environment suggests possible disorientation. Miss Lowens attempts to bring her back into contact with reality. "This is your dresser," she tells Miss Hansen. Mrs. Tomas relates to Miss Hansen as if the latter were in contact with her present reality. Do you agree with their handling of Miss Hansen's confusion?

7. Other patients suspect and accuse Miss Hansen of stealing. Miss Lowens tries to pacify them. She tells them that Miss Hansen is confused and should be given a chance to adjust. To what extent should other patients be told of a given patient's illness or background? Should a staff member express any evaluation of a patient's personality, *either* positive or negative, to other patients?

8. Miss Hansen's thefts and lack of bladder control disturb other patients. However, Mrs. Deil, the nursing supervisor, is reluctant to take action. She suggests a "wait and see" course of action. Do you agree?

9. What is your evaluation of the interview between Miss Hansen and Mrs. Deil? What problems could Mrs. Deil identify as a result of this conversation? Following the interview, Miss Hansen markedly regresses. What might have contributed to this reaction?

10. Dr. Torrey briefly answers the attendant's questions about Miss Hansen's condition. Do you feel his explanation is adequate? What else would you like to know about the case or the general problem?

11. Miss Hansen shows a motherly interest in and concern for other patients. What possible motivation can you suggest for this tendency on her part?

12. Some patients, particularly older patients, may constantly repeat stories of their past life. What might be the purpose of this kind of behavior? The staff may often be bored by and disinterested in these repetitions of familiar tales. Nevertheless, the patient has a need to express himself, to tell another about his life. How might a staff member direct such stories? What have been your feelings toward patients in similar situations?

13. Dr. Torrey suggests that efforts be made to involve Miss Hansen in useful activities. Miss Lowens acts upon this advice, but her efforts meet with failure. She experiences a feeling of helplessness. Why might she be making an unreasonable demand on herself and on the patient? Do you agree with Mrs. Deil's evaluation of the problem?

14. What special guidelines or procedures does your particular institution or hospital use in caring for geriatric patients? What suggestions would you make if you were

responsible for developing a plan of care and therapy for Miss Hansen?

15. Miss Hansen speaks of feeling lonely and of her fear of death. Miss Lowens talks about having faith and then tries to divert Miss Hansen away from her worries. What would you do in a similar situation? Redirecting a conversation away from sensitive areas is a technique frequently used. Why is this done? Do you feel that diverting a patient from a sensitive area reduces tension?

16. Is Miss Lowens successful in her attempts to force Miss Hansen back into reality by emphasizing immediate interests and concerns?

2

"I Just Got A Few Things To Settle"

Mrs. George Ryan telephoned the Community Mental Health Agency requesting an emergency visit from a nurse. She explained that a number of problems had arisen, and she would appreciate receiving some guidance. Four months ago she had returned from the hospital with a baby and had been under the supervision of a visiting nurse. The visits ended when the nurse and Mrs. Ryan felt that she was able to manage without further assistance. She had not been seen for a month and had placed the call because "Something has come up unexpected, and I feel like I'm going nuts." She pleaded for the same nurse or someone just like her to come right over and help straighten out the situation.

The secretary at the Agency probed for details, but Mrs. Ryan was evasive. She said that she was calling from a pay telephone and didn't have much time. "I just want someone over right away."

The matter was referred to the supervisor, who asked Miss Webster if she would stop and see Mrs. Ryan before making her scheduled visits in the same area. The nurse who had originally consulted with Mrs. Ryan was not available.

Miss Webster drove to the Palmetto Trailer Court, one

of several lining both sides of a four-lane highway near the edge of the city. She parked her car in a gravel lot at the entrance to the court and found Mrs. Ryan waiting at the door of the pay telephone next to the manager's office. She ran over to the car, asked if she were the visiting nurse, introduced herself, and asked Miss Webster to accompany her to the grocery store before they went back to the trailer.

"To the grocery store?" Miss Webster's tone reflected irritation.

"I got to get a carton of milk," explained Mrs. Ryan.

"It seems to me you could have done that before I came."

"I was afraid I would miss you. I been waiting here. I thought I'd go batty until you showed up."

"There wasn't any need to wait here. I'm sure I could
(1) have found your trailer. I'm pressed for time. You called and said there was an emergency, Mrs. Ryan. I rushed over and you tell me you are going shopping. This isn't a social visit."

"The grocery store is over next to the manager's office. He charges a lung for anything you get. But I'm only getting milk. Then we'll go to the trailer."

"I am not going shopping with you. You can tell me what you have to say right here and then you can do whatever you have to. Is there a problem with the baby? Where is your child?"

"I gave him to my girl friend while I came over to call."

"Is he ill?"

"No," said Mrs. Ryan. "He had a leaky nose last week, but now he's fine. He's not why I called. He's been fine. It's more than I can say for myself. But we got to hurry.

1. Before finding out the reason for Mrs. Ryan's behavior, the nurse reacts with irritation. While her response is understandable in terms of her busy schedule, it is certainly not conducive to establishing a helping relationship with a person undergoing stress.

Come with me to get the milk. Or you can wait here. I'll get the milk and run back."

"I'm not going with you and I think that I had better leave now. I told you I have a number of calls to make. This doesn't seem like an emergency."

"You got another guess coming," said Mrs. Ryan. "I got to get the milk. I can't go back unless I get something. I told him I needed milk. He gave me the money." She held out her hand and showed Miss Webster several coins. "If I go back there without milk, he'll raise the roof off the place. You see, I go back with milk, and you come in. I'll tell him I was down here and I met you on your way to Janie's – that's my girl friend – she had a baby a month ago. He knows that a nurse came here when I came back (2) from the hospital. He'll think you're the one coming to see Janie. You don't have to say nothing. Just stand here. Then we can sit down and visit and you can see for yourself. I got to have someone help me," she said desperately. "I been crying all morning. I bet I look like somethin' the cat dragged in."

"You look fine," said Miss Webster.

"Do I?" asked Mrs. Ryan. "That's not what Janie thinks. You should know the whole bit. I tell you, if it wasn't for Janie, I'd go out of my mind. We better hurry and get the milk."

Miss Webster accompanied Mrs. Ryan to the store. The milk was purchased, and they started back through a maze of lanes in the trailer court.

"We're way at the back," apologized Mrs. Ryan. "It's a new section. We got nothing but dirt," she said. "Here they got gardens and flowers." Each of the trailers was set in a small area on a cement platform surrounded by gardens

2. Mrs. Ryan is asking the nurse to participate in a deception, and one may wonder if deception is characteristic of the way Mrs. Ryan relates to her husband.

outlined with small picket fences to mark the property divisions between trailers.

"Our section's got troubles. I should have told the manager but I can go back later." She told Miss Webster that the new area shouldn't have been opened, but the manager was in a hurry to make a profit. They had trouble with the lights and sewage system. The power was continually failing. The septic tanks were overflowing. They had moved in three months ago, Mrs. Ryan reported, and had been waiting ever since to have their TV aerial hooked up. "That's how it started," she explained.

"What started?"

"I was just down watching TV. I told you we got no TV, and so I went down one night to my other girl friend's, and I took the baby because I didn't want to leave him alone. I left a note for George and told him I was over in Palmetto A – that's the first section. They got good reception there and my girl friend said to come down anytime, so I went down."

"And your husband?"

"Like I was telling you. He came home and he raised hell. He broke every dish we had. I got all those dishes with stamps I been saving for the past six months and every one broken." Mrs. Ryan began to cry. "I can't get control of myself," she apologized. "I'll get the baby. My girl friend lives here." Mrs. Ryan went into a trailer, got her son, and put him in a small carriage. "We're the last trailer," she told Miss Webster.

The Ryan trailer was a large, sixty-foot, silver trailer standing in an open area. Surrounding the trailer were empty cartons and boxes. Mrs. Ryan explained that everyone was just moving in, and the manager hadn't cleaned up the garbage. A sports car was parked alongside the trailer. "That's what he does with the money. He doesn't drink too much," she said scornfully. "He can't. He's paying off on the car. He makes good money," she told Miss Webster, "but he blows it in. I told him I wanted a new frig and he goes and gets the car. You should see the frig we got. My girl friend said maybe I shouldn't complain. It keeps the milk so hot you don't have to warm it for a bottle."

She knocked on the screen door, which had a large center hole. "He did that," she whispered to Miss Webster. "He must have been lit up. He said he thought he was hitting the door. He forgot there was a screen."

"George," called Mrs. Ryan. "You decent? I got someone with me. The nurse."

Mr. Ryan came to the door, stepping over cracked dishes which still littered the kitchen galley of the trailer. He opened the door; Mrs. Ryan entered and invited Miss Webster to follow.

* * *

Twenty-eight years of age, Mr. Ryan had been steadily employed at a local utilities company for the past ten years. He was now in charge of a crew installing gas pipes in a new housing development. The salary scale was excellent. In addition to his regular wages, the union had successfully bargained for substantial overtime pay. Mr. Ryan frequently spent extra hours on the job because of his increasing family expenses.

Elvina Ryan, his wife, was twenty years old. She had completed three years of high school before quitting at the legal age of sixteen to go to work in a diner which had opened to serve the large numbers of men assigned to the housing project. Mr. Ryan had gone to the diner for coffee each morning and met Elvina. After several months of steady dating, he asked her to marry him.

Elvina accepted readily. She told George that she was tired of working on her feet all day. She also told him that the other waitresses were envious because she had (3)
made such a good catch. George Ryan was a tall, muscular,

3. These comments suggest that Mrs. Ryan, at least inihandsome man who had been a popular customer among the waitresses. When he introduced Elvina to his mother, she told Elvina that she was probably making a mistake marrying George. According to the older Mrs. Ryan, George was "susceptible to temper." She added that aside from this defect, which he had had since he was a toddler, George was a pretty good son. Marriage, she said, might calm him down, but she wasn't predicting anything. Elvina dismissed the warning, feeling that her future mother-in-law was jealous and upset because, after they were married, George wouldn't be able to contribute half his earnings to her living expenses any more.

Elvina's parents were pleased about George. They saw him as an older husband who would "tame" Elvina, who had a tendency to be high-spirited. They encouraged her to marry without waiting too long and risking the possibility of George's losing interest. After Elvina and George were married, they lived in various furnished apartments until George surprised Elvina with the purchase of the trailer. He had returned to the one-room apartment one evening and presented Elvina with gold and blue sets of keys for her new home. They moved into the trailer the next day.

* * *

"What did she come for?" asked Mr. Ryan, pointing to the nurse.

"I told you, George, I bumped into her. Didn't I, Miss Webster? And she was going to Janie. Remember how I had a nurse come over after Dickie was born? That's going on now at Janie's."

tially, viewed her marriage as an escape from the drudgery of work, and that she seemed particularly concerned with the envious opinions of her friends. This hardly seems like an auspicious beginning for a stable marital relationship.

"You're a damn liar," George said. "What the hell did you come for?" he asked Miss Webster.

"I came, Mr. Ryan, because your wife called. It's our job to try and help. She's concerned about the baby and the family." 4

"So you didn't need no milk," Mr. Ryan accused her. "You went down sneaking to call. You told me you needed to get milk."

"All right, so I called," shouted Mrs. Ryan. "You're going to talk to her, George. You're going to let me talk to her. We got to. We got the baby."

"There's nothing to talk about," retorted Mr. Ryan.

"I would like to see the baby," said Miss Webster. She picked up the infant and cradled him in her arms. "He's a strong little fellow, Mr. Ryan. He's going to look like you. No you don't," she said, taking the baby's fingers. "Not my necklace. He's a darling baby," she told the Ryans. "He does have a wonderful color and you keep him beautifully clean."

"I'll make some coffee," said Mrs. Ryan.

"We're out of coffee," her husband told her.

"We're out of plenty," she muttered.

"I don't want any coffee," said Miss Webster.

Mr. Ryan told his wife to take the baby. He asked Miss Webster about her job, what she did, and whether or not the work was interesting. Miss Webster answered his ques- 5

4. Refusing to participate in Mrs. Ryan's deception, the nurse offers a straightforward, honest explanation of her visit. Although this leads to an immediate accusation by Mr. Ryan, the issue appears to be quickly resolved. In any event, continuing the deception initiated by Mrs. Ryan could hardly serve as an honest, secure basis for developing a relationship with the Ryan family.

5. By focusing attention on the visiting nurse, Mr. Ryan tries to avoid discussing his own problems.

tions briefly and stressed that she didn't come to talk about herself but had made the visit in the Ryans' interest.

"We got no problems," he told her. "We're fine."

"That's not true," said Mrs. Ryan. "He's supposed to take some medicine a doctor at the company gave him for his nerves. He should be taking it," she said.

Mr. Ryan took an ashtray from the table and flung it against the opposite wall. "You shut your damn mouth," he told his wife. "Ask her what the hell she's doing at night."

"I told you I was watching TV with the Mahons. They invited me."

"You can stay home."

"Why should I stay home? You don't."

"I was working."

"Until midnight?" she asked him. "You finish at ten."

"I stopped off for a couple of beers."

"Two hours," she said. "Two hours! How long does it take to drink two cans of beer?"

"None of your damn business what I was doing. What the hell were you doing at the Mahon's?"

"I told you," insisted Elvina. "I was watching TV with Doris."

"Yeah," said Mr. Ryan, standing up and going over to his wife. He grabbed her by the wrist and twisted her hand back. She screamed.

"You was watching TV with Doris. Then tell me how come Doris was with Jim having two beers with me? How come, I ask you? Doris got a twin?"

He dropped her wrist and Elvina crouched in a corner.
(6) "I went over to Doris's and she wasn't home so I went back to Janie's. I didn't want to tell you," she whimpered, "because you told me you don't like Janie."

6. The husband's suspiciousness is matched by his wife's deceptiveness, and his outbursts of aggression frighten her even more and lead to continued deception. Thus, they have fallen into a pattern of continuing conflict.

He kicked the broken dishes and walked out of the trailer, slamming the door.

"Can you make him go to a hospital or something?" pleaded Mrs. Ryan. "I'm scared. You saw the way he grabbed me," she whispered. "He said he would kill me and the kid if he ever found me out like that again. I tell you I was doing nothing. I was watching TV. I can't stand being stuck here alone so much. Before we was married I got out. We went to the movies. We went bowling regular, like once a week. I miss the league. I can't stand being here cooped up every night. I was a fool to fall for his line." She blamed her parents for pushing her into the marriage. "I'm stuck," she said, "and I'm scared he's going to hurt me and Dickie."

She told Miss Webster that sometimes George "got so mad you couldn't talk to him." During these outbursts he broke anything within his reach. Once he had taken a scissors and cut up her best dress.

Miss Webster urged her to seek immediate help.

"Like the police?" asked Mrs. Ryan.

Miss Webster said that was a decision Mrs. Ryan would have to make, but that she had been referring to psychological help available through the clinic's facilities.

"If I call the police, he'll kill me for sure," said Mrs. Ryan. "Look, maybe some it it is my fault. I don't want to get him in no real trouble – like with a police record. When he's calmed down, he's not a bad guy. He never does anything real mean except when he goes off the top of his head."

Miss Webster said that she would recommend family therapy. Mrs. Ryan readily agreed and asked Miss Webster to help her make arrangements and to please try and convince Mr. Ryan. "Maybe he'll listen to you if I'm not here." She took Dickie, went outside, and told Mr. Ryan that the nurse would like to talk to him. She pleaded with him to listen to the nurse. Mr. Ryan returned and sat slumped in the chair.

"What do you want?"

"I think you have some problems troubling your family

and I would like to see if we could get some help."

"Problems?" asked Mr. Ryan scornfully. "You kidding me or something?"

"I'm serious, Mr. Ryan."

"So am I," he said dully.

Miss Webster suggested that arrangements could be made for the Ryan family to be seen as outpatients at the clinic. (7) Mr. Ryan consented. He told Miss Webster that his wife and child meant a great deal to him. He said that nothing he did seemed to make Elvina happy. He blamed her friend Janie, who was always showing her things her husband bought and bragging about her various possessions. He said he often worked double-time to give his wife luxuries, but she was never satisfied. He had known how unhappy she was trying to keep house in a furnished room. He had gone heavily into debt to buy the trailer as a surprise. He hadn't told her about the purchase but had just driven over after the sale and handed her the keys. He had been terribly upset when she told him, "I'm not going to live in any goddamn trailer." Mr. Ryan was still bothered by memories of his wife's initial reaction. He had considered selling the trailer but "once you buy them, they're hell to unload. We're stuck here." He felt that after Elvina had moved in and made a few friends she seemed happier. "Trouble is she picks the wrong kind of friends. She's got taste in her left foot. Of all the people around here, she falls for the line that Janie hands out. I'll (8) bash her head in if she comes around. She knows to stay away when she sees me coming home."

Miss Webster said that unfortunately she couldn't remain

7. There is some suggestion here that his wife's rejection of his efforts to please her are interpreted by Mr. Ryan as a reflection on his adequacy as a person.

8. Seeing others as a bad influence, and thus placing the blame on Mrs. Ryan's friends, shifts the reponsibility for their problems out of the immediate context of their relationship.

and talk any longer with the Ryans because of previous appointments, but she urged both of them to apply for therapy. A visiting nurse would be able to see them together on a weekly basis to assist them in trying to work through some of their immediate problems.

Miss Webster asked Mr. Ryan about the medication his wife had mentioned. He said that it was some kind of drug the doctor over at the utility company had given him because sometimes his stomach got tied up in knots. "There is a lot of pressure," he explained. Occasionally he worked two shifts, which meant that he was on the job all day and part of the night with breaks only for coffee and meals.

"Are you taking the medication regularly?" asked Miss Webster.

"Hell, no," he told her. "I get so damn sleepy. Groggy. I pretty near lost an arm because of the stuff. My lids fell down like I was dopey. My mouth was dry – like my saliva was dust. I can't take no pills and do a decent job. I heard from a friend of mine that he bet I was taking tranquilizers. He said that's what they do to you. Like hell I need tranquilizers. I'm not one of those fags you see in pictures all tensed up."

Miss Webster urged Mr. Ryan to return to the doctor, since it was possible that he might require a different dosage, but Ryan said the best thing was not to take any drugs at all because he could manage. Miss Webster said that she wasn't questioning his ability to function; however, everyone went through some periods of stress. At those times, she noted, an outside viewpoint was important in helping individuals cope with problems that otherwise might be overwhelming.

"She's got problems, I know," he told Miss Webster. "I guess it's rough on her being alone so much with the kid." 9

9. Mr. Ryan shows a degree of sensitivity and insight which might be capitalized on in psychotherapy.

* * *

The Ryans did apply for therapy and were assigned to Miss Conner, a visiting psychiatric nurse who worked for the Community Agency. She arranged to see them in the morning before Mr. Ryan left for work. The Ryans greeted her cordially at the first visit. Mr. Ryan offered to make coffee and told his wife to make toast.

"Not so often do we get such a damn good-looker early in the morning for coffee. I just got done shaving," he apologized, checking his face in the mirror suspended on a wire over the sink. "The mirror is low. Who in the hell switched the mirror?" he shouted.

Elvina said she put it lower because she couldn't see herself when it was hung up near the cailing.

"All you got to do is twist it. You shouldn't have changed
(10) the nail." Mr. Ryan ripped the mirror from the wall and pulled out the nail. Several pieces of plasterboard came with it.

"You can't leave a damn thing around here without it being touched when your back is turned. I get so damn sick of this," he swore.

Elvina returned with coffee and toast. Miss Conner thanked her and asked how the family has been.

"Fine," said Mr. Ryan. "Fine. Great. No problems."

"You're lying," Mrs. Ryan told him. "You're lying. Sure, we got problems. Don't let him kid you," she told the nurse.

Miss Conner suggested they might like to discuss the problems with her. She asked what problems they found disturbing. "Have you been feeling low?"

"It's like a quiz show," answered Mr. Ryan. "Did you

10. A central issue, of course, is Mr. Ryan's lack of impulse control, and because of the potential danger involved, this issue is likely to color one's entire interpretation and treatment of this case.

train long for this job? You seem kind of young. Married?" 11

"I came to talk about you people," replied Miss Conner.

"Say," asked Mr. Ryan. "Haven't I seen you somewhere before? You ever been over at Roseland dance hall?"

"When the hell were you there?" askd Elvina.

"Before I got strangled with you," said Mr. Ryan. "What do you think I was doing until we met – counting dandelions? Lay off me, kid. You ever go to Roseland?" he asked Miss Conner.

"No," she said. "Perhaps, Mrs. Ryan, you might like to explore some of your feelings with me."

"I could tell you plenty," she said sullenly.

"So tell her," said Mr. Ryan. "Tell her you felt you got gipped. Tell her you got cheated. I give you money, bought 12
you the trailer, work my ass off so you can sit on your fanny and feel like you got rooked. Well, listen here, kid, let me tell you I got no prize in you."

The Ryans continued attacking each other. Several times Miss Conner tried to intervene and was told, "Keep your nose out of a private matter." They argued for an hour and Miss Conner got up to leave. Mr. Ryan expressed surprise that she had to leave and Miss Conner told him that she only came for an hour. He urged her to come on back for "a second installment."

The arguments continued during the next three sessions.

11. Once again trying to avoid discussing his own problems, Mr. Ryan shifts attention to the visiting nurse. In response, the nurse makes a rather abstract and general statement about exploring feelings rather than dealing with Mr. Ryan's concrete behavior within the context of their relationship.

12. This conversation provides further evidence that Mr. Ryan feels insecure about his own sense of adequacy, particularly in relation to his wife, and this leads to his verbal attack.

Miss Conner made repeated attempts to focus the conversation around their problems, but after a few words, the Ryans lapsed back into arguing with each other. Miss Conner discussed their behavior with her supervisor. She felt that they were very troubled and wondered if they should be seen separately. Their personal attacks on each other made therapy impossible. When either Mr. Ryan or Mrs. Ryan expressed any feeling about a subject, the other one would strike back with a hostile remark. Miss Conner cited examples from her last interview. The supervisor agreed that Miss Conner should introduce to them the possibility of individual therapy at the clinic.

At the next session, Mr. Ryan expressed a great deal of affection for his wife. He told Miss Conner that he worked long hours to earn extra money and looked forward to returning home and finding her waiting in the trailer. She was frequently absent. Mrs. Ryan insisted that she was visiting neighbors because she was lonely and wanted to watch TV. She told Miss Conner, "If I sit here alone night after night I'll lose my mind."

Mr. Ryan accused her of infidelity with other men. "I bet you do more than watch TV," he said sarcastically. His charge was emphatically denied by Mrs. Ryan.

"Then how come they know so much about us?" asked Ryan.

"They hear you shouting," said Mrs. Ryan. "You don't exactly whisper. You should hear him at night. I am waiting for the day when we're thrown out of here."

"Fat chance," answered Mr. Ryan. "I'll kill them if they try."

"He's always wanting to kill someone," she told Miss Conner.

"That might not be such a bad idea," he shouted.

"You're too chicken," Mrs. Ryan told him, picking up Dickie and walking out of the trailer.

"I get sick inside about the way she carries on when my back is turned," Mr. Ryan told Miss Conner when they were alone. "You got a boy friend?" he asked.

Miss Conner said she was engaged.

"I wonder how he would feel if he came over one night and found you in another man's house – like maybe someone he worked with."

Miss Conner said that Mrs. Ryan denied this kind of behavior and suggested that Mr. Ryan's accusations and suspicions were harmful to their relationship.

"She tells you she isn't messing around. But I got my own ideas."

Miss Conner asked Mr. Ryan if he would consider going to the clinic for individual therapy. She offered to help set up an appointment with one of the doctors. Both he and his wife needed help, she told him, and the clinic could offer this kind of service on an outpatient basis.

Mr. Ryan agreed that he would try anything because he was afraid of losing his wife and child. "I know I'd go out of my mind if I didn't have them. It's kind of hard for me to tell you what I feel. I come home shot. I drive up here (13)
thinking I'm going to see a light in the trailer. The place is dark. I know she isn't there, and all the while I'm driving home, I've been building up kind of a story that she'll be sitting – maybe waiting up with coffee for me. You get what I mean?"

* * *

Although Mr. and Mrs. Ryan consented to make appointments at the clinic for individual therapy, neither completed the application. Miss Conner drove over to the trailer court at the scheduled time of her visit and found Mrs. Ryan

13. Although Mr. Ryan's feelings of hostility are most obvious, he also feels dependent on and affectionate towards his wife. As a matter of fact, his dependency, affection, and sense of inadequacy are undoubtedly related to his suspiciousness and hostility.

sitting alone in her trailer weeping. Her face and arms were bruised. She told Miss Conner that her husband had beaten her the previous evening.

"I was over at my girl friend's watching TV when he came over. It was awful." Mrs. Ryan's hair was in disarray. She pointed to a bare patch on her scalp and told Miss Conner that her husband had dragged her by the hair and pulled some out. Her screams attracted the neighbors, who came but were unable to stop Mr. Ryan's assault. The manager telephoned the police, who came and got him.

Miss Conner asked where Mr. Ryan was, and Mrs. Ryan
14 said, "I don't care one damn. He can rot in prison. My God, imagine accusing me of fooling around with my girl friend's husband. All I was doing was sitting there watching the late movie. My girl friend had run over to her mother's because she was sick. She took her some food or something. She was coming right back. Ten minutes later and she would have been there, and maybe none of this would have happened."

Miss Conner repeated her suggestion that Mrs. Ryan telephone for an appointment at the clinic. Mrs. Ryan wondered what good that would do. "Say," she asked Miss Conner, "why are you so interested in us anyway? You know, I wonder if you got ideas about him." She accused Miss Conner of having more than a professional interest in her husband. "You can have him," she told Miss Conner. "Me – I'm going to get a lawyer and unload him. I've had enough."

* * *

According to the police report, Mr. Ryan had brutally attacked his wife. Two patrolmen subdued and handcuffed

14. Recognizing her husband's great concern about her visiting her girl friend, one wonders why Mrs. Ryan continues these visits – particularly at this time. She seems to be behaving in the way most likely to provoke his rage.

him and put him in the back of the patrol car. Mr. Ryan thrashed about, hysterical and confused. His distorted speech and convulsive sobbing prompted the police to take him directly to the emergency psychiatric unit at the county hospital, which maintained a twenty-four hour service.

The admitting nurse, Miss Leyden, telephoned for the resident on duty, who ordered a massive dose of a tranquilizer.

Mr. Ryan was placed in an office, still handcuffed, and a member of the hospital's security force stood guard. After about an hour, Mr. Ryan quieted down and asked if the handcuffs could be removed. The police were wary; however, Miss Leydon asked them to comply. She sat down at the desk to do an intake interview, asking the police and the hospital security officer to wait in the corridor.

"Troubles?" asked Miss Leyden.

"Yeah."

"Feeling better?"

"Some."

"Still a bit jumpy?"

"Kind of." What did they give me?"

"A tranquilizer. It's just to ease your tension," she told him.

"Acts pretty fast. Why a needle?"

"You could have taken the same medication in your mouth but then it would take time to go through your digestive tract," she explained. "The needle is the same medication but acts faster."

Mr. Ryan was satisfied with her explanation. He rubbed his eyes.

"Still feel kind of dazed?"

"Mostly sleepy," he replied.

According to hospital regulations, all patients, including those coming to emergency, were required to answer a number of questions. The intake interview schedule for emergency psychiatric patients included general personal data such as age, marital status, sex, address, etc., followed by a list of symptoms. The interview was conducted by a staff member who was supposed to ask the patient whether or not he had experienced any of fifty listed conditions, including hallucinations, suicidal feelings, nervousness, suspiciousness of others, hearing voices, restlessness, inability to sleep, migraine headaches, etc. On the right-hand side of the page, the staff member was asked to give a preliminary diagnosis to be confirmed by a doctor. Theoretically, the diagnosis was tentative, but there was some concern among the staff that the initial diagnosis tended to follow and label a patient. Usually the staff filled in "schizophrenic" or "paranoid" merely to simplify the problem of filling in the forms.

Miss Leyden proceeded to ask Mr. Ryan the individual
(15) items on the list. He murmured "Yeah," to every one. Several times he complained that his head hurt and asked to go to the bathroom. He was taken by the security officer. When he returned he continued his response of "Yeah" to every single symptom cited by Miss Leyden.

"Are you trying to think about each of these items before you answer yes or no? You've said 'yes' to all of them."

"I wasn't listening to you," admitted Mr. Ryan. "Can I call my wife? Did I hurt her bad? I didn't want to hurt her."

Miss Leyden said he could call his home, but Mr. Ryan then said it was impossible. He explained that he didn't have a telephone in his trailer and he was afraid of calling the manager's office in the middle of the night. He asked Miss Leyden to check for him the next morning.

"What's going to happen to me?" he asked.

"You probably will stay here for awhile."

"You mean locked up?"

"This is a hospital, Mr. Ryan. No one will lock you up."

15. Under heavy medication and clearly disturbed, this hardly seems an appropriate time to gather detailed psychological information about Mr. Ryan.

"I'm not hurt or nothing."

"You'll be up with patients who have problems – in the psychiatric unit," explained Miss Leyden.

"Crazy, you mean." At first he seemed stunned. Then he said, "Maybe I am. Maybe I am going nuts. I told my wife before I left that I wanted her home. I came back and she was gone. Once, just once, couldn't she have stayed there waiting like I said? That's all I wanted – her and me – when I came in. She wasn't there. And then I don't know what got into me. I couldn't stop myself."

The resident signed the form admitting Mr. Ryan to the psychiatric unit, and Miss Leyden, the hospital security officer, and a city policeman took him up. When the group reached the third floor, the night attendant on duty, Mr. Olsen, became worried.

"What are you bringing in at three in the morning? You know I got only one other person to help me."

Mr. Olsen told Miss Leyden that he couldn't manage without some help. Miss Leyden said that Mr. Ryan wasn't likely to act out. His charge was wife beating; he was on tranquilizers and was quite subdued.

"Maybe so," answered Mr. Olsen, "but maybe for tonight we put him in seclusion." He felt this was the only way that he could handle the case. In the morning the day staff could worry about Mr. Ryan, but Mr. Olsen was concerned about the possibility of having an entire ward awakened by the new arrival.

The handcuffs were removed and Mr. Ryan was placed in the seclusion room, a small barren room with a mattress on the floor. His personal effects and clothes were taken from him and he was left alone. Miss Leyden returned to the office with Mr. Olsen and expressed her displeasure with the arrangement. She told Mr. Olsen that she disapproved of his decision but had not wanted to challenge his authority in front of the patient: however, confinement to the seclusion room could only serve to heighten Mr. Ryan's anxiety.

"But meanwhile he's safe," said Mr. Olsen.

"I don't think you have to worry. He isn't going to hurt anyone here. He's angry at his wife, not us."

"You think he doesn't blame you or me? Come on now – off of it. I know the kind," said Mr. Olsen. "You got some idea he's some poor sad guy and all you need to do is to be sweet and then he'll be sweet as pie. I seen that type. He's
(16) got murder written all over him. Beat his wife. He's the kind that first chance he'll get, it'll be more than beating. You see his face? Now look. I got no help up here to speak of. We got to get through the night. Seclusion does those kinds of guys good. They get cooled off."

Miss Leyden strongly disagreed. She felt that Mr. Ryan was troubled and frightened and had been admitted to the hospital for help, not for punitive actions represented by seclusion or isolation in any form. "Our function," she told Mr. Olsen, "is to integrate patients into society, not to alienate them further." However, she was unable to get Mr. Olsen to change his mind.

The next morning, rumors circulated through the ward that a violent, dangerous convict had been brought in the previous night by the police. The patients, curious about the new patient, hovered near the seclusion room door and had to be directed away several times by Miss Charry, an attending nurse. But the patients wandered back and several were present when Mr. Ryan was brought out of the seclusion room.

* * *

The psychiatric unit of the county hospital consisted of thirty beds. Patients were kept for a maximum of sixty days before being assigned to other facilities or discharged to be

16. Although placing Mr. Ryan in seclusion at this point may or may not be appropriate, the attendant's decision would seem to be influenced more by his own fears than by a concern for the patient.

treated on an outpatient basis. The majority of the patients were referrals either from the general emergency room or the emergency walk-in psychiatric clinic maintained by the hospital. Many of the patients were brought to the hospital by friends, family, or in some cases, by the police. Because the psychiatric ward did place a limitation on the amount of time a patient could remain, long-range therapy plans were not possible. Treatment generally consisted of drugs and informal therapeutic interviews.

One staff member felt the measures employed didn't do anything for the patients, but kept them out of harm, away from their families and outside stress. He also felt that patients were discharged when the staff knew they would be back again for second and third rounds. "But what can you do? We can't lock everyone up."

The staff consisted of nurses, attendants, social workers, occupational therapists, and resident psychiatrists and psychologists, many of whom were in training on a part-time basis. Plans were being developed to provide short-term, intensive therapy through team operations.

* * *

The next morning, when Mr. Ryan was released from seclusion, he was quiet and polite to the nurse. He said he had been upset when he was locked up that way, but when he thought it over, he realized that the staff thought he might hurt someone.

"I'm not that kind of guy," he assured the nurse, Miss Charry. "I know it might look like that because of what I did. But it was the first time." He asked Miss Charry if she could help him make a phone call to his wife. She didn't know where he was and he didn't want her to worry.

A call was placed to the Palmetto Trailer Court, and the manager said a message would be delivered to Mrs. Ryan. While waiting for his wife to call back, Mr. Ryan wandered around the corridors. He attempted to speak to other pa-

(17) tients but they backed off. He reported to Miss Charry that he had overheard the patients calling him some kind of murderer. He was quite upset and asked her if he looked like that kind of guy. He said it was making him nervous to think that he had some kind of reputation that wasn't justified.

Miss Charry and he sat down and talked, and Mr. Ryan told her that he had been having some problems with his wife. "Nothing serious," he stated, but she had got him upset and he kind of pulled her hair. He thought that he had lost his temper because she had said he was hurting her and all he was trying to do was make her come home where she belonged. He was very sorry about what had happened and desperately wanted to apologize to his wife. He asked Miss Charry to try to contact his wife. A second call to the trailer court was placed, and Miss Charry was told by the manager that the message had been delivered. There was nothing he could do about making Mrs. Ryan respond.

Miss Charry asked Mr. Ryan to sit down and continue to talk with her. His behavior was extremely subdued and Miss Charry felt that he appeared embarrassed when the conversation revolved around his behavior toward his wife. In fact, he seemed to Miss Charry not only contrite but depressed and withdrawn in any discussion concerning his wife. He became more alert, however, when they talked about general topics, such as his job and the current problems involved in working with his crew. At that point, Mr. Ryan realized he hadn't phoned the utility company, and he asked for permission to call his boss.

The detached and depressed manner Mr. Ryan showed in his conversation suggested to Miss Charry that perhaps

17. As in any group living together, rumors in a psychiatric ward can play an important part in labeling a new patient. Being labeled violent and dangerous in turn influences the behavior and experience of the patient.

he was receiving too heavy a dose of tranquilizers. She felt that the dosage should be changed. Mr. Ryan's reaction after he made the call to his company confirmed this impression. He sat gripping the sides of his chair and crying, telling her he couldn't remember the last time he ever cried. He was worried about his job. He had never been sick and hadn't missed a regular working day in the past five years. He felt "like hell" asking for sick leave when he didn't feel he was sick – "not in the way the company sees being sick."

He also told Miss Charry that he was sleepy and that wasn't like him. He didn't like feeling sleepy and the sensation of having his eyes close on him against his will. "I'm the kind of guy who can go twenty-four hours without a break and here I'm talking to you and I can't keep my eyes open." He wondered if the medicine he was taking was too much for him.

Later that afternoon, Miss Charry spoke to one of the residents about Mr. Ryan, whom she described as an intelligent young man who had been admitted for attacking his wife. She reported that it was Mr. Ryan's first hospitalization and that he had not been under previous psychiatric treatment except for a few sessions in family therapy. She said she felt that the dosages of tranquilizers being given to Mr. Ryan were too high, that they were making him sleepy and uncomfortable. He had asked for the prescription to be changed, and Miss Charry thought this advisable, since it seemed difficult to reach him when he was under heavy sedation. She didn't feel that he was a violent man. He was (18)
hard-working and very much concerned about his wife, his

18. While others may overly emphasize the violent and dangerous aspects of Mr. Ryan's behavior, the nurse seems to discount and rationalize Mr. Ryan's hostility. Although seeing him only in terms of dangerous violence is not likely to be very helpful to Mr. Ryan, failure to recognize and appreciate the potential danger is unrealistic and certainly child, and his job. Because of economic pressures, he had been working two shifts and was reaching a point of exhaustion. She thought his explosive attack on his wife might have been a consequence of his fatigue. It was the first and only time, he had asserted, that he had ever laid a hand on his wife.

The psychiatric resident, Dr. Wallin, disagreed. He had read the several reports and a description of Mr. Ryan's behavior with the police and felt that, until they knew more about the case, Mr. Ryan should be treated as potentially violent and that the dosage should be kept at the same level.

Miss Charry dissented, maintaining that Mr. Ryan wasn't the type of man to be dangerous. Dr. Wallin, on the other hand, felt that the nursing staff assumed that as long as a man was compliant on the floor, he was basically good. He certainly wasn't suggesting that Mr. Ryan was a criminal, but he felt that they should wait and observe his behavior before reducing his dosage. "There is one fact in the case we have to accept. According to the police, five minutes later and there would have been a double murder—his wife and the baby. You didn't know that he beat the infant, too? It's in the police report. I don't think I can look at this case as just a matter of a man's being tired when he comes home from work. I have a feeling there's more to the story."

Two days after Mr. Ryan was admitted to the hospital, his wife visited him, bringing a suitcase with changes of clothing for him. He was excited at her arrival and called the nurses and attendants over to meet her. She told him that she couldn't stay long because she had left the baby with Janie and had to get back, but Mr. Ryan insisted that she talk with him. He wanted to apologize and turned to Miss Charry for verification. "Isn't that what I been saying every day? I want to apologize. I was tired. It was too hard

not therapeutic. One-sided and narrow interpretations of any patient's behavior are rarely helpful either to the patient or to others concerned.

working two shifts."

"I'm going to stay home more," he told her.

Mrs. Ryan said she hoped so. She touched the top of her hair and said her scalp hurt where he had pulled out her hair.

He begged her not to make him feel worse than he did.

"It's not me so much," she told him, "but Dickie. You busted Dickie's arm. You didn't know that? Didn't anyone tell you? The kid has been crying night and day. Busted the baby's arm," she told Miss Charry.

"You're going to let me back," he pleaded.

"I can't say for sure, George. It depends. I been doing a lot of thinking. How long you going to be here?"

"They tell me it won't be long." He turned to Miss Charry and asked her if she had any idea how long he would have to remain hospitalized.

Miss Charry said that it would depend on how he felt and how the doctors assessed his case.

"It can't be more than a week – not the way I feel. How's everything been?"

"So-so," she told him.

"Is Dickie OK now?"

"What do you expect? He's got a cast on his arm."

"Will he be OK?"

"I guess so. I might not grow hair back here," she said pointing to her head.

"Sure it will come back."

"Maybe not."

"You still angry at me?" he asked her.

"I guess not, George. I guess I don't care much except it's got to be different."

He promised her that it would be different when he returned home. Miss Charry left, and Mr. Ryan walked his wife to the elevator. He asked her about his car and asked her to start it every day so the battery wouldn't run down.

"I got to use the car," she told him. "It's just sitting there. I got to drive Dickie to the doctor's."

"Can't you take a bus?"

19 "With the car there, George? It's just sitting there."

"You leave it alone," he told her. "You don't touch the car. That's my car," he said. He took her hand and squeezed it and she winced under the pressure. "Don't you touch the car," he warned her.

"What'll you do to me, if I do, George? How will you know? You going to kill me, George?" she taunted him.

After she left, Mr. Ryan told Miss Charry he felt bad telling his wife about his car, but he was worried because she had just learned to drive and he didn't want her getting hurt. It was a powerful sports car and she hadn't much experience driving in the city. She had never driven his car before, and he was sure she hadn't any idea how to shift or use it properly.

That evening Mr. Ryan tried to leave the hospital. He was stopped by an attendant at a rear elevator. The attendant barred his way, and Mr. Ryan insisted on being allowed to pass. The attendant said that Mr. Ryan could not leave the hospital without permission and Mr. Ryan said, "I can damn well get out of here when I want to. It isn't a jail." The elevator stopped at the floor; the doors opened and Mr. Ryan tried to enter, pushing his way past the attendant. The attendant took Mr. Ryan's wrists and pulled him back. They struggled, and the attendant shouted for assistance. Mr. Ryan swung the attendant around and pushed him against the wall. Two other attendants came and restrained Mr. Ryan.

The resident was summoned. Mr. Ryan told Dr. Wallin that he was not aware that he had to have a pass to leave the building. As far as he knew, he was voluntarily in the hospital and could leave. The struggle with the attendant

19. Mr. Ryan's car apparently has some special psychological meaning for him. One wonders if the car is associated symbolically with his sense of adequacy.

had been a misunderstanding, he insisted, and he had hit the attendant in self-defense. "I don't like no one hitting me," he told Dr. Wallin. "I'm not hot about using my fists, but when I'm attacked I don't stand back and take it." The doctor explained to Mr. Ryan that he must have a pass before he could leave the hospital.

Mr. Ryan asked for a one-day pass to go home and see how everything was going. His request was discussed at a case conference. Dr. Wallin listened to the nurses' reports. Miss Charry said that Mr. Ryan should be allowed to go home. She described his wife's visit and how upset he had been when he heard about his son's broken arm. "He craves affection from his wife," Miss Charry said. She felt that the couple needed to be together so that Mr. Ryan could express his feelings to her. She felt that Mr. Ryan was aware of his problems, eager to be helped, and would benefit by a brief period alone with his wife.

The attendant described Mr. Ryan's attack, insisting that he was the kind who "goes off his rocker and is blind when he gets mad." He didn't know why, but intuitively he didn't trust him. "That guy Ryan has a temper. He's supposed to be on drugs and you should have seen him boiling over when he got one idea in mind and I crossed him up."

Dr. Wallin admitted that he had mixed feelings. On the one hand, he recognized Miss Charry's arguments, and on the other he saw the attendant's viewpoint. He had talked with the patient, who had insisted that he had a right to leave. Although Mr. Ryan had had no part in the original decision to hospitalize him, he certainly had a legal right to leave now. "When I told him he had to apply for a pass, he was amenable and said he was sorry that he hadn't known. Otherwise, the misunderstanding with the attendant could have been avoided."

Considering the family and the child, the group felt that a one-day pass should be given with the understanding that George was to return to the hospital at six o'clock.

George was most appreciative when he heard the decision.

"It's what I need. Just a few hours," he told Miss Charry. "A few hours." He snapped his fingers. "I been here four days, and it seems like a year already. One day – take care of a few things and then back again. Right," he told her.

"Take it easy," the attendant told him.

"Sure thing," said George. "I just got a few things to settle – just a few things, and then I'll come back."

"I JUST GOT A FEW THINGS TO SETTLE"

1. Miss Webster displays annoyance with Mrs. Ryan, who wants her to go to the store to purchase milk. Was the nurse justified in telling Mrs. Ryan, "This is not a social visit?" In assessing a situation, there must be attention given to both verbal and nonverbal cues. In your opinion has Miss Webster attended to information other than the verbal comments of Mrs. Ryan?

2. On the walk back to the trailer, Mrs. Ryan superficially discusses some of her concerns. What does she reveal about her relationship with her husband? Think of a situation in which a family member expressed negative or positive feelings about another person you had not met. Do you recall whether these feelings influenced your attitudes?

3. Mr. and Mrs. Ryan quarrel, and Miss Webster attempts to divert them by paying attention to the baby. Do you believe this was a good way to short-circuit the arguing? What effect does this technique have on the expression of feeling? Was Miss Webster successful in this instance?

4. Mr. Ryan describes his feelings toward his wife. What are some of the resentments he harbors toward Mrs. Ryan? In considering the interpretation given by Mrs. Ryan and the feelings presented by Mr. Ryan, how might you characterize their relationship?

5. Mr. Ryan perceives Miss Conner as attractive. Discuss how the age, sex, appearance, and social class of the staff members may affect the development of therapeutic relationships. Have you found any particular type of patient resistant to your help? What characteristics in yourself do you feel that patient might have been reacting to?

6. Miss Conner is unsuccessful in dealing with the Ryans together. Do you agree with her about the reasons for her inability to develop rapport? Think of situations where you felt family therapy was successful. How were these situations different from the Ryans'?

7. Mr. Ryan threatens to kill the manager of the trailer court if he is dispossessed. How meaningful a threat did that appear to you?

8. Mrs. Ryan hints that Miss Conner may intend to seduce her husband. How would you handle an accusation such as this?

9. Miss Leyden is brief and to the point during her intake interview with Mr. Ryan. Was her style appropriate to the situation? Discuss different styles of behavior appropriate to this type of situation.

10. Intake interviews such as the one described here are widely used in practice. Has your institution found them helpful? What other methods might be used for diagnostic purposes? Describe any experiences you have had with other procedures.

11. What difficulties may arise when patients are labelled with a diagnostic category upon hospital admittance?

12. Miss Leyden does not wish to contradict Mr. Olson's authority in front of Mr. Ryan. Do you agree? Can you describe a situation where you have countermanded an order of another staff member in the patient's presence? Describe the circumstances and the effect on staff rela-

tionships. In this instance would you have intervened or waited as Miss Leyden did to express disapproval?

13. Mr. Olson reacts intuitively to Mr. Ryan and feels that he is dangerous. Although intuition may seriously be questioned as lacking objectivity and being unscientific, nonetheless intuitive judgments frequently influence attitudes. Awareness of one's self and one's attitudes can help check intuitive reactions. Try to think of certain types of patients toward whom you felt an immediate intuitive response. Have you been wrong? To what degree has your intuition had a certain validity?

14. The use of seclusion as a controlling or punitive device is frequently employed. What are your feelings about the use of restraints? What effects have you observed in patients subjected to such treatment? What was the effect on Mr. Ryan?

15. Miss Charry and Dr. Wallin perceive Mr. Ryan from two opposing viewpoints. What are the reactions and attitudes characteristic of these distinctly different perceptions? What is the evidence presented to justify each of the viewpoints?

16. How does Miss Charry's viewpoint influence her conviction that George Ryan should be permitted a one-day pass? Once a judgment is made about a patient, it can be difficult to reassess the situation. What might one do to help keep an open, nonjudgmental attitude?

3

Rock To A Silent Beat

Hospital records concerning Margie Rariton were incomplete. Admitted on a court order with a tentative diagnosis of adolescent character disorder, the only information regarding her background consisted of brief chronological data. Records showed that from the age of five until fourteen she lived in a children's shelter. When she reached adolescence, her disruptive behaviors led the staff to believe that she might benefit more from the security of a family atmosphere in a foster home. The first placement was unsuccessful, and the family requested that she be removed. Other foster homes were tried, but each attempt met with failure, and the shelter was compelled to take her back. However, she continued to be disruptive and was placed under the jurisdiction of the Children's Court. A summary statement of interviews with court officials, a social worker, and a psychologist stated: "Margie, fifteen years old, is depressed, withdrawn, sullen, and unresponsive." Psychiatric treatment was recommended, and she was sent to a state psychiatric hospital for diagnostic testing and therapy.

Mondaro Hospital, located about twenty miles from a large metropolitan city, consisted of eight buildings situated on extensive grounds. Until recently the hospital had been administered through one central office; however, increases in staff and patient population had made organizational changes necessary. The hospital retained its name, but when Margie arrived, each building was functioning as an autonomous unit with its own director and staff.

Margie was brought to the hospital by a social worker. She remained silent during the intake interview, forcing the social worker to answer all questions by referring to Margie's court folder. At the conclusion of the interview, the social worker expressed confidence in Margie's ability to adjust to the hospital environment.

Margie's response was a plea to go home.

"You're going to stay here until you get better," replied the social worker.

"I want to go home," repeated Margie.

She reluctantly picked up her small suitcase and portable radio and accompanied the nurse to the fourth floor of Building Three, an adult unit of male and female patients with a variety of psychiatric disorders. Since none on the floor were severely disturbed, limited mobility was permitted. Weekend passes were routinely granted for visits to families or others who would assume responsibility for the patients' care.

Margie's entrance into the female wing of the floor was immediately observed by other patients. Although she said nothing, obediently followed the nurse and unpacked her few possessions, patients stopped at the door and came into the room to stare at her. She was a remarkably attractive adolescent with a slight but developed figure distinctly outlined by snug pants and fitted sweater. Long thick hair reached to her waist. Although she wore heavy makeup, the powder, lipstick, rouge, and eye shadow could not distort the delicacy of her features.

During the first weeks of hospitalization, Margie continually paced the corridors, holding a portable radio close to her ear. Throughout the day she listened to music. At night the radio was propped up on a pillow, and Margie fell asleep, a sheet drawn over her head, one ear pressed against the radio's small speaker. (1)

Efforts on the part of the nursing staff to relate to Margie were rebuffed. She responded either by turning away or staring at the nurse with a wide unblinking stare. Miss Namm was disturbed by Margie's resistance. In the past she had had considerable success relating to adolescents assigned to the floor, probably because she was young and the patients could identify with her, or at least feel they were understood. She experimented with a number of different approaches with Margie, attempting to discuss clothes, makeup, boys, all topics which most adolescents were willing to talk about. None met with any response.

"How can you talk to her with that radio going full blast?" complained Miss Namm to Mrs. Darion. "She doesn't listen."

Mrs. Darion, who had been nursing supervisor on the floor for the past ten years, discussed Margie's behavior at a case conference. Margie was being seen by a psychiatrist and was being tested by the psychologist. Until more definitive information regarding her diagnosis was available, Mrs. Darion wondered if the staff should stop trying to force Margie to relate to them. "She doesn't seem ready to talk to people." The staff agreed. Miss Namm said that she had already decided to sit back and wait until Margie came to her. "It's pointless to keep after her."

At the beginning of the third week, Margie came running down to the nurse's station holding a silent radio in both hands.

1. Without further information, it is impossible to understand fully the psychological dynamics underlying Margie's apparent attachment to the radio. However, it does have the obvious effect of blocking communication with others, and perhaps it also serves to block Margie's own self-reflection or communication with herself.

"It doesn't work," she cried.

"What doesn't work, Margie?" asked Miss Namm, pointedly avoiding the radio.

"My radio," shouted Margie. "Someone broke it." She shook the radio, pulled off the back plate, stared at the interior, twisted the dials, and held it to her ear. "There's no sound. Listen," she said, holding out the radio.

"I believe you. But no one touched the radio. We have to expect this to happen. Batteries wear out."

"It was a new radio," insisted Margie.

"But you've had it going steadily for two weeks. That radio has never been turned off."

"But radios can do that."

"That depends on the radio," answered Miss Namm. "Obviously yours couldn't."

"Will you fix it?" pleaded Margie.

"I don't know anything about radios."

"Do you know anyone? Isn't there anyone who can fix the radio?"

"We don't have anyone around here. It might very well need a new battery."

"That's it," said Margie. "Could you get me one?"

(2) "I'm sorry Margie. We can't get you a new battery."

"What will I do?" Margie's voice was a whine.

"What would *you* like to do?"

"Get my radio working. I've got to have it. Don't you see I've got to have it?" Margie gripped the radio in one hand, tried it again, then smashed it to the floor and ran back to her room.

Miss Namm picked up the battered parts of the radio.

2. In view of the frustration represented by the radio, the nurse's reaction surely is understandable. But regardless of one's evaluation of her action, it would seem that the nurse might also have recognized the patient's feelings in this incident.

Margie's aggressive action was noted in the records and reported to Mrs. Darion. Mrs. Darion felt that Margie's symbolic destruction of the radio that had been a block to communication was a breakthrough.

"She was so attached to that radio. It was a crutch. I've never seen a girl that age attached to something like that. She was totally dependent on the radio. Maybe now we can reach her without trying to talk above it!"

That afternoon Mrs. Darion went over to Margie, who was seated in the patient lounge, legs drawn up to her chest, her chin resting on her knees. Her left cheek was thrust out into a round ball. Margie's jaws moved steadily as she chewed a large wad of gum. The left cheek flattened; the right swelled. Puckering her lips, Margie blew an enormous bubble which she punctured with a scarlet fingernail before sucking the gum slowly back into her mouth.

"It's a lovely day, Margie. You haven't been outside since you've come. Would you like to go out for some exercise with the other patients? They're going to play volleyball." (3)

"I don't like volleyball. I hate volleyball," answered Margie.

"You don't like volleyball? All girls enjoy volleyball. When I was your age, Margie, we played volleyball all the time."

"I said I hate volleyball. Anyhow, my name's not Margie."

"Then you could take a walk or do something else. I'll talk to Miss Ellen and see what other game she could suggest. Of course your name is Margie. Margie Rariton. I know that Margie is short for Marjorie. Do you know that you have the same name as my best friend in nursing school? She called herself Margie, too. If I had my choice of names,

3. The nurse is encouraging Margie to join in the activities of other patients, but Margie is apparently resisting. Rather than continue her efforts to persuade Margie to join the game, the nurse might have been more effective if she had attended to Margie's feelings, trying to understand the basis of her behavior.

that's the name I would choose. But then we don't have a choice. Names are gifts from our parents. Now then, how about volleyball?"

"My name is Lillian." She removed the gum from her mouth, tossed it to the floor and stamped on it with her heel. Taking a package of cigarettes from the pocket of her jeans, she took one, lit it, stood up, and leaning against the wall, inhaled deeply.

"Not on the floor. Gum is a nightmare to remove. Here's a tissue."

"Do it yourself."

"It's already stuck. Please don't keep stepping on it. Your name is Marjorie on the records. Marjorie Rariton, and we will call you Margie, if you wish."

Margie tossed the half smoked cigarette to the floor.

"You can't do that Margie. You're going to lose smoking privileges. This is dangerous. Pick it up."

"You're going to call me Lillian."

"I'm going to call you Margie because that is your name.
4 And you're going to pick up that cigarette and put it out in an ashtray. After that, you will give me the matches in your pocket. When you want a light from now on you will have to ask one of the staff. You may not have matches. Matches are a privilege you must earn."

Mrs. Darion mentioned Margie's denial of her real name to Miss Namm, suggesting that Margie certainly might have schizoid tendencies which the nursing staff should be made aware of. "She kept insisting that her name was Lillian."

Miss Namm felt that Margie could be called whatever

4. Rather than trying to understand the motivation for Margie's name change, the nurse insists that Margie face reality. A conflict develops, Margie blatantly breaks the hospital's rules, and a potentially important opportunity for understanding the patient and communicating this understanding to her has been lost.

she wanted to be called as long as she didn't burn the place down. "We can work on the name problem, but if she sets the hospital on fire we won't be able to worry whether her name is Margie or Lillian. Did you tell her that she can't keep matches? Is there anything in her history about arson?"

When Miss Namm went into the hall, Margie was waiting for her. In all previous encounters Miss Namm had been the first to greet Margie. This time Margie pointedly called out to Miss Namm and asked if she might talk with her.

"Everybody's so old here," said Margie wistfully. "I wish there was someone more my own age. You're not very old. I mean you're not that much older than I am."

Laughing and chatting about ages, Miss Namm thanked Margie for her compliments and the two of them sat down together to talk. Miss Namm was surprised that every question she asked was met with a direct response and a smile.

"The other nurse is pretty angry at me," said Margie.

"She's worried about fires. I can't blame her. We wouldn't want the place to burn down," Miss Namm said in a teasing voice. Margie laughed spontaneously.

"I guess I got kind of burned up myself. She's such an old dog," said Margie.

"But you can't blame her, can you, Margie? You must know how dangerous it is to drop a cigarette."

"You sound like the sisters at the Home giving me a lecture," giggled Margie.

"I'm not lecturing and I'm not going to make you stop the habit."

"You can't," interrupted Margie.

"I didn't say we would, but you are smoking far too much and you're only hurting yourself. But that's up to you. Meanwhile, I am concerned about your dropping lighted cigarettes on the floor."

"It was the first time – I forgot, truly." Margie twisted her long hair into a curl and coyly drew it under her chin, "I'll remember." She held out several books of matches. "Would you keep them for me? I'm sorry for what I did. You may have them. You can look through my things. I don't have any more. Do you want to hold my cigarettes, too?" She held out a package of cigarettes.

"We trust you, Margie. Mrs. Darion said that you wanted to be called Lillian. Is that right? I'll try and call you that from now on."

"I don't care. If it's hard for everyone to remember, just say Margie," she replied softly.

Margie's sudden swing of mood from hostility to angelic cooperativeness disturbed Miss Namm. She felt that Margie should be watched, feeling suspicious about the behavioral changes, which she suspected were manipulative maneuvers.

The first concrete information about Margie's background was provided by Sister Ann from the St. Mary's Children's Shelter. On a visit to the hospital, Sister Ann discussed Marjorie's background with Mrs. Darion.

"She was brought to the shelter when she was five. There were three children, a little brother almost one, and an older brother who was about eleven."

"By her mother?"

"No, a case worker brought them. The children weren't up for adoption. They never have been. It's a shame though, because the little ones were so precious. I believe the father lived somewhere in New York. We never knew exactly where the mother was," said Sister Ann sadly. "She lives in Florida now."

"What was Marjorie like as a child?"

"Beautiful, just beautiful. She was so winning," reminisced Sister Ann with fondness. "Everyone adored her. That's what was so hard for all of us to understand as she grew older. She had so much attention from everyone and then she would change so."

"Maybe that's the problem," said Mrs. Darion.

"Too much attention?"

"No, being so attractive. She didn't have to do anything else. She just was pretty and that seemed to be enough."

"Oh, no," said Sister Ann. "She was very good. When she was only a little one, I would have her helping me with the younger ones and they loved her. Her character was developing beautifully. It was only recently that she seemed to change so much."

"How do you mean?"

"It wasn't anything that clear," said Sister Ann. "She would be good one minute and the next minute you couldn't talk to her. Then, too, we have boys and girls at the home, and Margie became interested in the boys. It's difficult when you have a large group to handle, and we do have so many children to care for. The foster families loved her. They all offered the same reason for not being able to keep her. They were sorry about having to give her up. She was such a lovely looking youngster."

"What was the reason?"

"They worried about her moodiness. I gather it wasn't anything specific, but just her way of being an angel one minute and then gloomy and miserable the next. It's a responsibility being a foster parent and in Margie's case there were fears about her getting into trouble. She had a habit of starting out one way and then right in the middle she turned on the people who tried very hard with her. I often asked her why and she said someone inside made her do that. I really shouldn't say any more," added Sister Ann. "I know all of you here know much more than I do. But it was always so hard for me to understand why she turned on people who cared about her. Just when everything seemed to be going well, she would do something upsetting. I do hope she doesn't do that here."

Mrs. Darion told Margie that Sister Ann had come to visit her. Margie's response was an indifferent shrug of her shoulders.

"Sister Ann has come a long way. She has gone to a great deal of trouble to see you, Margie."

5 "I didn't ask her to come."

"I wonder if that's the right attitude, Margie. She has made an effort to see you. She is very fond of you and from what she told me, you got along well together. Don't you think it would be thoughtful if you saw her? I think she would be very disappointed if I went back and had to tell her you didn't want to see her."

"What does she want?"

"I didn't ask her. I assume she wants to find out how you are doing. Why don't you talk to her yourself?" answered Mrs. Darion.

"Does she want to take me back to the home?"

"Why do you say that?"

"Why else would she come? She's the one who always came to take me from the foster homes."

"No, you're going to stay here with us for awhile. Sister Ann is waiting, I know she has to get back. Don't disappoint her."

Margie lit a cigarette.

"Why don't you smoke later?" said Mrs. Darion.

"She knows I smoke," responded Margie.

After several minutes of reflection, Margie agreed to see Sister Ann, and she returned to the Nursing Office with Mrs. Darion.

Mrs. Darion left the room and Sister Ann and Margie talked familiarly about children and staff in the Home. Margie was eager to hear about what had happened to a number of the youngsters with whom she had lived. When Sister Ann told her that one of her former friends had been living in

5. Given her history of early and repeated rejection, much of Margie's behavior is likely to revolve around her concern about whether or not people sincerely care about her. Thus her behavior may alternate from trying to win other people's attention and affection to testing them as a way of determining if they really care about her.

a foster home for six months and was going to a regular school, Margie said she was happy and would like the girl's address.

"It would be fun to write to her. Bet she doesn't get too many letters from a mental hospital," Margie said sarcastically.

Sister Ann said she would send the address. "Now I do have news," she added. "I have two letters. You're going to be very pleased with this one." She gave Margie a letter from her younger brother.

"I told him I was coming to see you and he wanted to write a letter. I knew you'd be happy to hear from him. His handwriting still needs improvement, but he is proud because he wrote it all himself."

The letter said, "Dear Margie, I hope you are getting better in the hospital. Sister Ann said you weren't feeling well. Did you have your tonsils out? I had a party for being ten. We had cake and soda. I pray for you. Your brother, Richie."

"Isn't that a darling letter, Margie? I told him you were in the hospital but he wasn't to worry."

"You didn't tell him what kind of a hospital?" 6

"No I didn't," replied Sister Ann.

"Why?"

"I don't think he's old enough to understand, Margie. You see, sometimes all of us have moments in life when everything isn't as it should be. We need help just as you are getting help. But Richie is young and I didn't feel this could be explained to him."

"You don't want him to know I am in a nut house."

6. Her recurrent experiences of rejection are most likely to result in a sense of self-worthlessness. Being hospitalized may reinforce this feeling, and Sister Ann's apparent reluctance to let Margie's brother know where she is may well be interpreted by her as further evidence that she should be ashamed of herself.

"That's not it at all, Margie. It would be nice if you wrote a letter to him."

"I'll think about it," said Margie.

Sister Ann reached into her handbag and withdrew a second letter. "This one is the real surprise. It is addressed to me but I want to share it with you. My, this letter was unexpected. It has been many years since I heard from your dear older brother. Would you like to read it yourself?"

"No!"

Sister Ann opened the letter. "His handwriting has improved," she commented. "Dear Sister Ann, I am living in Florida with Mom. She had me come out last spring. I wrote to her. Jobs were tough up north so I came down here. She sent me a bus ticket. I am living with her now but later maybe I'll get my own place. I thought about going back to school. They got a good mechanic school in town. I can work at a garage and go to school. It sounds like a good deal. I told Mom about the kids, Margie and Richie. She's glad they are doing good. I told her Margie was in the hospital and she got worried. I told her it was nothing but Margie got off the beam but she'll be OK. Mom says maybe next year if she keeps the job (she's working at a diner) maybe she'll have Margie down. She'll let you know and you can tell Margie. Mom said to find out how Richie is doing. She bets she wouldn't recognize him. He must be a big kid. If you can, write the news to me at General Delivery, Bradentown, Florida. P.S. Tell Sister Angela I don't get up at six. Boy, do I remember her."

"They are all thinking of you, Margie," said Sister Ann. "Would you like to keep the letters? I know you would. You're in my thoughts and prayers." She patted Margie's hand. "I'll try and come again."

(7) "Can you take me out of here?" asked Margie.

"No, I can't do that," answered Sister Ann. "It's best that

7. Margie's request probably reflects another test of whether or not someone else cares for her, and of course, once you stay here for a while, but I do promise I'll come and visit soon."

"Don't bother," said Margie.

Before leaving, Sister Ann reported the conversation to Mrs. Darion. She said that she was concerned about Margie's attitude. Although the girl had always been fond of her younger brother, she seemed to show little interest in his letter. Her interest in the older brother's letter had been minimal, but then Sister Ann wondered if this might be explained by the fact that Margie and Tom had not seen each other for several years or more. Sister Ann also reported that Margie had been generally warm and pleasant, but at the end of the visit, when she had told Margie she would come again, Margie had replied, "Don't bother."

That afternoon Margie went out with the patients for the regular recreational hour. She declined an invitation to participate in the volleyball game, preferring to walk around the fenced enclosure picking up twigs and leaves, stuffing them in her pocket. Mrs. Perkins, a middle-aged attendant who had been on the staff for many years, spoke with her and joined her in the stroll.

At the end of the period the patients were called together and formed a straggling line. Escorted by attendants, nurses, and recreation leaders, they returned to the hospital, entering through a rear basement door. After reaching the fourth floor ward, Miss Namm checked off the roster, at which point Margie's absence was noted. Mrs. Darion ordered an inmediate search of the grounds.

Mr. Aston, a maintenance worker, and Mrs. Perkins located Margie behind the hospital incinerator, fanning the flames of a small fire she had built. When he approached, she screamed at him to remain away, a command which he ignored. When he did come closer, Margie dropped the

again she is likely to interpret Sister Ann's response as a rejection.

8 two letters on the flames. Mrs. Perkins talked to Margie while Mr. Aston stamped out the fire with a shovel.

"You're going to burn the place down," said Mrs. Perkins.

"Good," shouted Margie.

"That's not so good," said Mrs. Perkins. "You know we got people here. We got jobs here. Don't you go making fires again. You told me you wanted matches to take a smoke. Now I gave you matches and look what you did. You come on back now like a good girl and don't give us any more trouble. You hear?"

Mrs. Darion was extremely annoyed that Margie had been given matches, a privilege which had been taken away from her after the first incidents involving cigarettes. She questioned the staff, and Mrs. Perkins admitted that she had given the matches to Margie.

"You had no business giving her matches," said Mrs. Darion. "She is not to have matches."

"How was I to know?" asked Mrs. Perkins.

"I told the staff," said Mrs. Darion.

"Who did you tell?"

Mrs. Darion did not answer, and Mrs. Perkins pressed for an explanation. "I asked, who did you tell? You told the nurses," she said. "Who handles the patients around here? Don't you go blaming me about those matches. You know we work with these people and they got a problem and you don't tell us, so how are we going to know?"

Discussion of the incident continued during the staff meeting on the following day. Mrs. Darion commented on Margie's action and the potential dangers of arson. She stressed the fact that under no circumstances should Margie

8. It is important to note the symbolic meaning of Margie's burning of the two letters. These are letters from two people who left her and who most likely represent painful rejections in her life. Burning the letters may be a small but significant revenge. Unfortunately, the staff's realistic concern about fire obscures the question of why Margie behaved as she did.

be permitted to have any matches.

"Why?" asked Mrs. Pekins.

"She has demonstrated that she can't be trusted. There is the hazard of fire. This is dangerous."

"You don't have to tell me that," argued Mrs. Perkins. "I got that message but I want to know why?"

"What do you mean?" asked Dr. Armel.

"I mean exactly what I said. You know something about Margie. You tell us she shouldn't have matches. OK, I want to know why. I understand she likes to play with fires. I don't want the place burned down, but I want to know why she plays with fires."

"There are many ramifications to the case," said Dr. Armel. "We haven't any conclusive diagnosis at this point, but we're (9) hopeful that some clues to her behavior will be revealed as time goes on. I hope we can share some of our findings at that point."

"Don't tell me that," said Mrs. Perkins. "I know you've been seeing her. I know she's got a whole fat case record, and I know that there must be something you can tell me so's we can work with her."

"I believe that if you just follow the policy of no matches as we suggested, that should be enough at the moment," answered Mrs. Darion. "As Dr. Armel said, when we know more, we'll tell you."

Mrs. Perkins remained dissatisfied. After the psychiatrist left the meeting, Mrs. Perkins told Mrs. Darion and the remaining staff that it wasn't right that the attendants had no access to a patient's case records. "It's the attendants who

9. In this instance, the psychiatrist probably doesn't know much more than anyone else about why Margie started the fire, but rather than openly admit his lack of understanding, he retreats with a vague statement about ramifications and implied complexities. The attendant, on the other hand, feels the psychiatrist knows more than she does, but won't share his knowledge. Conflict and misunderstanding arise from a lack of open and honest communication.

are with the patients all day. When do they see the doctor and the nurses? They see them at certain times and in private – who's with them all the rest of the twenty-four hours? You tell me that we got to work in the dark. I say we shouldn't work in the dark. There are patient records. We can't see them even though we're responsible. Don't you think we could get an idea what to do if we saw those records?"

The psychologist said that Mrs. Perkins shouldn't be upset. "Most patient records are pretty vague anyhow. No one really reads them in detail."

"Then what do you people do all that writing and spend the time locking the file drawers for? That's no answer," said Mrs. Perkins.

"The files are closed," began Mrs. Darion, "because they have confidential material about the patient's behavior and personal history."

"Isn't that just the kind of information we should have?" asked Mrs. Perkins.

"Not necessarily."

"What do you mean not necessarily!" exclaimed Mrs. Perkins. "There is plenty there. I would have known Margie was dangerous with matches. Don't you know I've been around here long enough, handling every kind from the one who'll rip your hair out to the one who won't get out of bed to go to the toilet even if it means messing the bed? Don't tell me if I didn't know something from the records I couldn't know better why patients act like they do! How you think we can work in the dark beats me. Maybe I say something that is wrong to a patient. If I had known what was in those records, I would have kept my mouth shut. Maybe I would see those records and know that one patient needs some extra attention, then I could go ahead and spend time. But if I don't know what's in the records I do nothing. That's not right."

"Let me tell you something else," she went on. "One day they needed some help in downstairs administration. One of (10) the girls who files took sick, so they had me go down. I tell you now I didn't get much filing done that day. I read through closed records. I sat there all day and I read, and I learned a lot. I remember reading about Mr. Cantrece, a patient up here at the time. He was a devil, let me tell you. You couldn't walk near him without him exploding, and he had other habits that made us all sick. Then I read in those files about him. You know he had no family; they all was killed in an auto accident. OK, I read more, but when I came back to the floor I couldn't get mad at him any more. Don't tell me knowing what's in those files don't make no (11) difference."

"The cases are reviewed at staff meetings," replied Mrs. Darion.

"You think that's enough? We go through each one and someone says something and somebody else says something, but the pieces don't always fit. It's like a puzzle. You can say all you want, but you know that the records should be read, and we should be doing the reading because we're the people who deal with the patients."

Mrs. Darion said that Margie's records weren't complete

10. Mrs. Perkins is unquestionably making a valid point about a problem which derives, in part, from the typically hierarchical structure of hospital organization. This does not necessarily mean that the basic structure need be changed; but it does suggest that the communication problems involved in the organization must be clarified and resolved. Otherwise, the structure itself is likely to breed suspicion, communication will be faulty, and the entire process of patient care will suffer.

11. This instance dramatically illustrates the importance of understanding the reasons underlying a patient's behavior.

12 and therefore would probably be of little value in interpreting or analyzing her behavior.

"It's not only Margie," said Mrs. Perkins. "You know that. I'm using Margie as an example. I gave her those matches. If I had seen the records, I would have knowed it wasn't the right thing to do. But how was I supposed to know?"

Mrs. Perkins remained dissatisfied with the explanations given her for not permitting attendants or aides to have access to the records. "They know it and we know it," she told several attendants over coffee. "This place would stop running if it wasn't for us. But what kind of a job can you do when they hide those records? We're the ones who handle the patients."

Mrs. Perkins told Margie that it had been wrong for her to take the matches, particularly when she knew that she wasn't to have them. "You're supposed to ask when you want a light. You can't go around burning up the place."

"I wasn't burning up the place," insisted Margie. "I was just burning some letters."

"Why didn't you throw them in the wastebasket?"

"I wanted to burn them."

Margie apologized for having upset Mrs. Perkins, and from that time on she pointedly requested lights for her cigarettes only from Mrs. Perkins. After striking the match, she would insert the cover in the flap and hand it back.

"There's nothing wrong with that kid," commented Mrs. Perkins at the next staff meeting, as she reported Margie's recent behavior.

On Friday afternoon, as Mrs. Perkins was getting ready to leave, Margie approached and asked for a match.

"Where are you going?" she asked Mrs. Perkins.

12. Mrs. Darion appears to be more immediately concerned with the argument than trying to understand and resolve the real problem that is involved.

"Home for the weekend."

"Do you live far?"

"Not too bad," said Mrs. Perkins. "Maybe twenty, twenty-five minutes – depends on the traffic. Friday's the worst."

"Do you live alone?"

"No, I have two kids."

"And your husband?"

"I'm divorced."

"I'm sorry."

"I'm not," said Mrs. Perkins. "My kids are better off. I have a boy your age and a girl a year younger."

Margie walked Mrs. Perkins to the door.

"I haven't been anywhere since I've been here," said Margie wistfully. (13)

"Don't you get passes?"

"I suppose so," answered Margie, "But you have to have a place to go."

"Don't you have no place to go? Family? Some friends?"

Margie shook her head.

"Not this weekend," said Mrs. Perkins, "but maybe another weekend I'll take you home with me. Would you like that?"

The following weekend Mrs. Perkins mentioned to Mrs. Darion that Margie had asked if she could accompany Mrs. Perkins home for the weekend.

"She doesn't seem all that bad to me," said Mrs. Perkins. "I could manage her. She has really been an angel with me.

13. Once again, Margie is asking a person, "Do you care?" And of course the denial is most likely to be experienced by Margie as rejection. The central issue, of course, is not whether Margie is realistic in her wish to be taken home by Mrs. Perkins, but rather, the psychological meaning of this experience for Margie. Mrs. Perkins can hardly be expected to take home every patient who wants to visit her, but given the realistic and practical limits of the hospital setting, it is important to recognize the patient's needs and wishes.

I kind of feel for her being shut up and no place to go."

Permission was not given. Mrs. Darion said that it was unfortunate that Margie's hopes had been raised, but it was most unwise to have Mrs. Perkins take her home. Margie
(14) had obviously "worked on" Mrs. Perkins' sympathies. Her model behavior in relation to Mrs. Perkins had been a maneuver for special attention and favors.

Margie brought up the subject with Miss Namm after a group theraphy session and asked why she had been denied permission to leave for the weekend.

"I wanted to go," said Margie.

"I wonder if you might tell me why, Margie. Only a short time before you were angry with Mrs. Perkins about the matches."

"I'm not angry any more."

"Is that reason enough to want to go home with her?"

"Yes."

"Why do you really want to go with her?"

"No special reason."

"There must be a reason."

"I wanted to go home with her, that's all," shouted Margie. "She said she'd take me. I want to go home."

(15) "Mrs. Perkins' home is *not* your home, Margie."

"I want to go home with her anyway."

"There's a difference, Margie. You mean that you would like to visit Mrs. Perkins."

14. Although Mrs. Darion's interpretation is probably valid insofar as Margie's behavior was indeed manipulative, there is also a need to consider the motivation for Margie's manipulation.

15. Of course, Mrs. Perkins' home is not Margie's home, as Margie very well knows. At this point, underscoring the reality that she has no home is not what she needs. Rather, she needs someone who will empathize with her feelings of being homeless, alone, and rejected.

"I want to go home," whimpered Margie. "My name is not Margie," she said, slumping to the floor. "My name's not Margie. I hate all of you here. I hate it. I want to go home. What have I done to you?"

"Nothing, Margie. We're all very fond of you."

"You hate me."

"We don't hate you, Margie. We want to help you."

"Haven't I been good about the matches?" she pleaded.

"Yes."

"Look, I haven't any matches." She pulled out the pockets of her jeans. "They're empty."

"You don't have to prove that to me. I know we can trust you."

"Can I go home?"

"Home, Margie? What do you mean?"

"Home, home, home," Margie repeated, rocking back and forth on the floor. "Lillian wants to go home."

Margie was given a sedative and returned to her room to rest. When she awakened, she asked Miss Namm if the parts of her radio had been thrown away. Miss Namm said they had been saved and Margie asked if she might have them and perhaps try and see if the radio could be repaired. The parts were given to her, and Margie placed them underneath her bed.

That evening she asked the nurse on duty if it were possible for her to borrow some stationery and envelopes. These were provided, and Margie spent the evening writing letters. She did not seal the letters and the next day gave them to Mrs. Darion to read, with the excuse that she wanted the spelling checked. She also asked if they could be mailed because she did not have any money for stamps.

The content of all the letters was similar, expressing an interest in the other person, a statement of how happy and well she was, and concluding with a plea to be asked to visit until the court settled her permanently in a foster home. The letters were addressed to Sister Ann and to each of the four foster homes where she had lived for brief periods.

16 "Are they all right?" asked Margie.

"They're very nice letters."

"Just nice?"

"They are lovely letters, and I know the people will be glad to hear how happy you are."

"Will they believe that?"

"Don't you want them to?"

Margie ignored this question and asked Mrs. Darion if she felt that any of the people would answer her letters. "Will I be able to go and visit if they say yes?"

"We can discuss this when an invitation comes."

"This isn't the same as Mrs. Perkins. These people know me. You'll let me go if they ask. You can't make me stay here if they come and get me. You'll have to let me go. You'll have to let me go to visit," insisted Margie.

Sister Ann wrote to Margie and to Mrs. Darion. She explained to the latter that it would be impossible to have Margie visit and hoped that Margie wouldn't be too disappointed. She also said that the various foster parents had phoned and had told Sister Ann they were not responding to Margie's letter because they couldn't agree to her request and did not know what excuse to give her. Each, however, asked Sister Ann to convey their warm regards and hope that Margie was feeling better. Sister Ann had not written to Margie about these calls but asked Mrs. Darion to do what she thought best under the circumstances.

That afternoon Margie jubilantly greeted Mrs. Darion in the hall. "I'm going to need a pass."

"A pass?"

"For the weekend." Margie patted her pocket. "I got an answer."

16. Margie is again reaching out to others, and the tragic quality of her life is reflected here in that the ways in which she reaches out are doomed to failure.

"What did the letter say, Margie?"

"It said they would come and get me."

"Who is going to come, Margie?"

"One of the foster people I lived with. You don't know them."

"May I see the letter?"

"It's personal," said Margie.

"Do you want to tell me about them?"

Margie took out a crumpled cigarette and asked Mrs. Darion for a match.

"They were a swell family," said Margie inhaling deeply. "They liked me. The father kept telling me I was like one of his own daughters. They would have kept me except their son came home from the army. They only had three bed rooms. There was no room. I couldn't go into the girls-room – there were two little girls – so they called Sister Ann to take me back to the home."

"You liked that family the best?"

"It was awful leaving them. I saw the son. They even had me at the party when he came home. He told me if he had known I was going to be put out he would have done something. But there was nothing he could do. It was too late. He said he maybe was going back to college, and then I could take his room again."

During a subsequent staff meeting, Mrs. Darion discussed Margie's hope of being invited for a weekend visit. "Margie told me she had an invitation," reported Mrs. Darion, "but I find this hard to believe. I heard from Sister Ann yesterday, and she said that the foster parents had called her and said they would not invite Margie to visit. In fact, they weren't even going to answer her letter. Now maybe one of them did. Does anyone remember if Margie received two letters sometime this week – one from Sister Ann and one from someone else?"

"I know for sure she only got one," said Mrs. Perkins. "She was something. I thought she'd hit the ceiling. She told me she wrote a bunch of letters and that Sister Ann was the only one who answered. She showed me the letter and kept saying how stupid Sister Ann writes. There was nothing in that letter about going anywhere to visit."

"One thing is clear to me," said Mrs. Darion, "and that is
(17) Margie's imagination is running wild. Remember how she is with the names. Sometimes she wants to be called Lillian and insists that Lillian is her real name. She told me about a family coming to get her this weekend. According to her, they would have kept her but they didn't have enough bedrooms."

The discussion centered around whether the staff should play along with Margie's fantasy or confront her with reality. They decided that acceptance of reality was a problem with which Margie was struggling. It was agreed, however, that if the staff forced Margie to acknowledge the rejection of the foster families she would lose what little trust she had in them. In two days her illusory world would be shattered naturally. No one would come to the hospital to take her on a weekend pass. At that point, the staff could intervene if necessary and be supportive. The action to be taken would depend on Margie's reaction.

On Friday morning Margie washed her hair, dressed in a form-fitting skirt and sweater, and packed an overnight case. She went into the patient dayroom and sat waiting expectantly for her visitors. She refused lunch, explaining that if she ate a big lunch she wouldn't be able to eat the dinner that the family had said they were preparing for her visit. Late in the afternoon, Margie was still sitting in the lounge, smoking, a vague smile on her face. Mrs. Darion checked several times and Margie told her, as she told other

17. Yes, Margie's imagination is running wild. But given her history of rejection and her desperate need for others there can be little mystery about her need for a wild imagination.

staff members who inquired, that she was just fine and still waiting.

"They have a long way to come and they got held up in traffic."

"How do you know?" asked Miss Namm.

"They called the hospital to tell me," replied Margie.

At six Margie was still waiting.

Before she left for the day, Mrs. Darion spoke with the night staff and told them to keep an eye on Margie. "She expected people to come. She might be upset. In the event of any outbursts PRN medication can be administered and attention given to her."

Late Friday night Margie Rariton was sexually molested by a male patient who had a previous court record for molestation. (18) He had been hospitalized for six weeks and had been a model patient until the incident with Margie. The two were discovered by several elderly patients who screamed for help. Two attendants, Miss Laws and Mr. Canday, responded. The regulations of behavior for staff in such situations stated that staff would not use any physical action but should attempt to make the patients stop through verbal commands. The rationale was that patients at such times might become violent. The attendants were not successful. The male patient stopped them at knife point and they left the room seeking other staff assistance.

When they returned, the young man submissively returned to the male ward under the supervision of Mr. Canday. Miss Laws took charge of Margie, who showed no apparent reaction.

The entire floor, however, was in a turmoil. Older women patients who had been told of what had occurred became hysterical and demanded that doors be bolted and windows

18. Although there is not enough evidence available to make a confident interpretation, this incident probably is another instance reflecting Margie's general need to achieve some kind of relationship with another person.

locked. They frantically drew chairs to block their bedroom doors. Several, weeping uncontrollably, required sedation.

Margie shared a ward room with six other women, none of whom would permit her back into the room. Miss Laws could not reason with them, and Margie's bedding was removed and taken down to the nurse's office.

Saturday morning, the weekend supervisor, Miss Lemar, was told of what had happened. She questioned each staff member for information.

"Was the door locked?"

Mr. Canday insisted that the door to the male ward had been locked.

"Did any staff member leave the ward? Perhaps patients sneaked out."

"Not to my knowledge."

"Where were your keys?"

"In my pocket. I always keep the keys in my pocket." Mr. Canday showed Miss Lemar a ring filled with keys.

(19) "It beats me how he got out," said Mr. Canday. The floor had been remarkably quiet. All patients had been in their rooms during a bed check. Mr. Canday and the other attendants had been in the nurse's station.

"Was there any time someone wasn't there?"

"One of us was always on duty."

Miss Laws' report to Miss Lemar was similar to Mr. Canday's. All the patients had been quiet. Margie had been told to go to bed. "She had been expecting people," said Miss Laws, "but they didn't show up. She didn't act like she was

19. There seems to be greater concern with hospital regulations and determining which doors were locked than with the patient. Obviously, no hospital can effectively help patients without systematic regulations and appropriate safeguards. But focusing on these regulations and on assigning blame for possible transgressions can get in the way of understanding and helping others.

upset any. I told her maybe they would come the next day and she said that was an idea and she took it well and I saw her go off to her room."

As far as Miss Laws could recall, someone had been at the nurses' station in the corridor the entire evening. The glassed cubicle which served as the nurses' post provided a view of the corridor and a view of the front door.

She admitted that she had left her keys on the desk while she answered the telephone, but it was only a second and it was unlikely that Margie could have taken the keys, or if she had, it was doubtful that she could have identified the key which unlocked the main door separating the wards.

The attending psychiatrist was telephoned and informed. He asked how Margie was responding and was told that she had been given a sedative and was quiet. He asked to be called again in the event that her behavior changed markedly.

Mrs. Darion was informed about the attack on Monday morning. The administrative director of the hospital called an emergency staff meeting, and stressed that such incidents must not occur. New regulations were to be put into immediate effect. The director indicated that he had been aware that the night staff read and played cards while on duty.

"Because we haven't had any incidents like this for several years," he said, "we've been lulled into a false sense of security. Keys are not to be left on desks. It is wrong to assume that a patient doesn't know which key belongs to which door. They notice more than you think they do."

Miss Namm felt that the male patient might not be completely at fault. She mentioned that Margie, a stunningly beautiful, well-developed teenager, relied on her beauty to win favors from the staff.

"The fact that she didn't resist," mentioned Mrs. Darion, "leads me to believe that she might have provoked the man's attentions."

"There's no point in assigning blame," said Dr. Armel.

Several of the staff said that they were grateful that it hadn't happened to one of the older women. As it was, many elderly patients were still quivering and gossiping about the event. It was felt that Margie's youth might save her from any trauma. The final point made by the administrator was that the matter should not be discussed publicly. Dr. Armel would talk to Margie and the young man during the regular therapy sessions.

The assistant to the director, who was present at the meeting, was extremely upset. Recently, the hospital had received unfavorable publicity because of staff shortages. "Now all that has to happen is for the newspapers to pick this up," he said. "I'm worried about headlines – Teenager Attacked in State Mental Hospital." They'll paint some picture of this place as a hotbed of sex – just at the time we're putting in for a big budget increase. We can't have this happen again."

When Mrs. Darion returned to the floor, Mrs. Perkins told her, "Margie isn't too good. She seems worried. She keeps saying she might be pregnant."

"She's not the only one who's worried," answered Mrs. Darion. "This has upset everyone around here. How are the other patients?"

"They're getting over it," replied Mrs. Perkins. "Only Miss Calder, that little old lady, keeps running down to the door screaming, 'Is it locked'? She stands testing the door. I swear she's going to pull off the door handle."

Mrs. Darion went to Margie's room. Margie was sitting on the floor handling the parts of her radio. She held the broken speaker to her ear.

"How are you feeling, Margie?"

"My name's Lillian," whispered Margie.

"All right, Lillian. How are you feeling?"

Margie shook the speaker, settled it against her ear and swayed, smiling, as if she were listening to actual sounds.

"Is the radio working?" said Mrs. Darion.

"It's all fixed now," said Margie. "Would you like to listen?"

"No, I believe you, Lillian."

"They came," said Margie.

"Who?"

"The family."

"When did they come?"

"Friday. You didn't think they were really going to come, did you?"

"I didn't know."

"You thought I was lying."

"No, Lillian."

"They came like they promised," said Margie. "They wouldn't let me down. I was so good at that family's. I said to myself when I went there I would be good. This time I would be so good they wouldn't send me away. I told Sister Ann I would try. She asked me to try. She said she would pray for me that I would make it. It wasn't my fault in the other places. It wasn't. I told Sister Ann that Mrs. Harris – she's the first foster mother – slapped me and I got mad, but I told Sister that nothing would happen this time. Sister said it might be my last chance, and I tried. You don't know how I tried. It was going so well. They told me I was wonderful. They told me I was a beautiful girl. It wasn't my fault they sent me away. They hadn't known their son would be getting out of the army. They didn't have any room. It wasn't because of anything I did. That's why they would come here like they promised. I knew they would if I wrote."

Margie held the broken speaker to her ear, rocking to a silent beat. "Lillian's home now," whispered Margie to herself.

ROCK TO A SILENT BEAT

1. Rebuffed in her attemps to relate to Margie, Miss Namm ascribes her failure to Margie's devotion to the radio. Patients may employ various techniques to keep the staff at a distance. In Margie's case, an object is used as a barrier to communication. Can you give examples of other patient behaviors you may have encountered which have blocked communication?

2. Margie resists any attempt of the staff to establish a relationship. The staff feels they should withdraw and wait until Margie comes to them. What other measures might a staff member employ in trying to work with Margie? Do you agree with the decision to retreat and allow Margie to make the first overture? What might this procedure mean to Margie? Might this have implications for future therapy?

3. Margie is obviously attached to the radio. Knowing this, should Miss Namm have made an effort to get it repaired? What do you think motivated Miss Namm to refuse Margie's plea to fix the broken radio?

4. A frequent technique in trying to develop rapport with a patient involves establishing some common ground – the personal touch. Thus, Mrs. Darion admires the name Margie and notes that it is the same name as her best friend. Evaluate this technique. Discuss the drawbacks and the advantages. Margie insists that her name is Lillian. Why do you feel she wants to be called by a different name?

5. Margie challenges Miss Darion by refusing to pick up the gum and cigarettes she had dropped on the floor. What might have motivated Margie's behavior?

6. Miss Namm interprets Margie's mood swings to purposeful manipulation. Do you agree with this interpretation of Margie's motivation? What cues did Miss Namm employ to make this inference?

7. Can you give examples of situations where you felt you were being used by a patient? What was your reaction? How did your feelings influence your subsequent behavior towards the patient?

8. Mrs. Darion asks Margie to see Sister Ann. What does she say to convince Margie? What is your impression of the way this situation is handled? In view of Margie's reluctance, would you insist that she see Sister Ann?

9. What useful background information does Sister Ann provide that might help in understanding Margie's behavior?

10. Sister Ann's relaying of messages from her family appears motivated by good intentions. However, one problem disturbing Margie is the feeling of being rejected. Considering Margie's background and lack of family relationships, what might Margie feel after having heard the contents of the letters?

11. The effects of a family visit to a patient may be complex. It would be interesting to plot patient moods before and after visits from outsiders or family. How could such information help a staff member in relating to a patient?

12. Unaware of Margie's carelessness with matches and burning cigarettes, Mrs. Perkins gives Margie matches. Communication lines between staff members are not always clear. Mrs. Perkins feels that information is frequently withheld from the attendants, and yet they are the people who work directly with patients. What is your reaction? Do you feel that patient records should be made available to any staff member who has direct contact with a given patient? What would be the positive and negative aspects of such a system? Discuss different plans you may have encountered for opening channels of communication among staff members.

13. Permission for Margie to visit Mrs. Perkins was not granted. What effect does this have on Margie's subsequent behavior?

14. Are you in accord with the staff's decision to wait and let Margie's fantasy world be shattered naturally? Would direct intervention at that moment – confronting Margie with the facts – have altered the situation that developed?

15. Miss Namm's interpretation of the events suggests that Margie might have initiated the seduction. What is your feeling?

16. Although the staff feels that Margie may be less traumatized by the experience than would an older, more mature woman, is this necessarily true? How was Margie affected by the seduction?

17. Mrs. Darion begins to try and relate to Margie on the latter's terms. Do you think it is important for a staff member to speak and react on the patient's fantasy level? What are the possible problems which may result when the therapist begins to speak and respond in terms of the patient's private world?

4

"Of All People—Not David"

Mr. David Finkler, forty-four years of age, voluntarily committed himself to Le Claire Hospital on the advice of his family physician. During the intake interview with Miss Donahue he found it difficult to answer her questions. He said that he was very tired and didn't feel much like talking. (1)

"The words are stuck," he told Miss Donahue, pointing to his throat. "Stuck." He opened his mouth to continue speaking, but no sounds came out. Closing his lips, he smiled sadly. Tears came to his eyes. Miss Donahue handed him a tissue; he wiped his eyes and his perspiring forehead.

"You're feeling pretty tight inside?" asked Miss Donahue.

"Uh huh," replied Mr. Finkler. "Tired, tired." He pronounced the words as if each sound was independent.

"Would you say that you have been feeling tired most of the time?"

"Un huh." Mr. Finkler covered his face with his hands to

1. General fatigue and inability to speak are common symptoms of depression. These symptoms can have psychogenic causes, but they also may be a consequence of physical illness. It is therefore important to evaluate possible physical causes of the patient's symptoms.

avoid further questioning. They sat in silence. Mr. Finkler uncovered his face and folded his hands in his lap.

"You understand how I feel?" he asked her.

"Certainly," said Miss Donahue. She put aside the interview form and arranged to have Mr. Finkler taken upstairs to the psychiatric ward. (2)

Mrs. Finkler, who was seated in the reception room, patted her husband's arm and told him not to worry about anything except getting better. She assured him that she would be back to visit him that evening. After Mr. Finkler left with an attendant, Mrs. Finkler asked to speak to Miss Donahue. She expressed great concern about her husband.

"He's a sick man. What can I say – a sick man. It's the God's truth, if you asked me if something like this would happen to David, I would have told you you were crazy. Of all people – not David."

"Has he been depressed for long?" asked Miss Donahue.

"Maybe two, maybe three months. I kept telling myself it was nothing, maybe a cold or his stomach. To tell the truth, I thought he was getting better. His appetite was better, and then suddenly he talked about not wanting to live." (3)

"What happened?" asked Miss Donahue.

2. The nurse conducting the intake interview is sensitive to the patient's feelings of distress and recognizes that obtaining detailed information at this point is inappropriate. Case history data are necessary for making diagnostic decisions, but in this case, it is more important to admit the patient as rapidly as possible. A more detailed history can be obtained later.

3. It is not at all unusual for people to interpret symptoms of psychological depression in terms of possible physical illnesses. In fact, symptoms of psychogenically based depression are often superficially the same as those associated with relatively common physical illnesses.

"Don't ask," said Mrs. Finkler. "I can't talk about it. Thank God the doctor came. Tell me," she asked Miss Donahue, "is it possible that a man can live a whole life and be happy, and then something like this happens?"

"He was happy?"

"Happy!" repeated Mrs. Finkler. "Happy is not the word for David. Let me tell you, David was a happy man. We had our ups and downs, who doesn't? But David managed. If you ask me, I should be the one having a nervous breakdown. I am the one who sees kids stealing candy, and I get a pain like a stab in my heart. David – he doesn't notice. Our ice cream freezer in the store broke down. Everything was ruined. I got such a headache like a wire around my head. David looks at the mess. He says to me, 'Forget it – it's only ice cream.' Everything was spoiled. We lost, don't ask how much money, and David tells me that it's only ice cream. David is not the one to have a nervous breakdown. I tell you, I wouldn't tell one customer about David. They (4)
would never believe me. The world could fall apart, and David would smile. That was David."

Three months previously, Mrs. Finkler had insisted that her husband consult their family doctor. Gradually, over a period of time, he had become increasingly listless and unresponsive. There were no specific symptoms other than general malaise and fatigue. Always a man to rise at six to open their candy store at seven, he became unable to mobilize himself, and Mrs. Finkler had to open the store and take in the newspapers. During the day, Mr. Finkler felt he needed to nap. He had difficulty keeping his eyes

4. Early signs of depression may go unnoticed, particularly if the person generally tends to be passive and quiet. In contrast to the more obvious acting out behavior associated with some other psychiatric syndromes, the reduced activity level of early depression may not be socially disruptive and thus is less likely to elicit concern from others.

open and became confused and distracted. When Mrs. Finkler asked him about his problems, he said he felt low, and that nothing seemed to matter to him any more. He couldn't
(5) care less if the ice cream freezer broke down or if the newspapers stayed out in the rain.

"Does it matter," he told his wife, "if you don't read the papers? So who cares?" His attitude caused considerable anxiety to Mrs. Finkler. "You can't run a business," she told Miss Donahue, "and not care." David's indifferent behavior threatened the family with financial ruin.

* * *

For the past twenty-four years, ever since his marriage, David Finkler had operated a neighborhood store that stayed open seven days a week, from early morning until ten p. m. The store offered greeting cards, inexpensive novelty items, newspapers, magazines, small toys, school supplies, and candy. Half the store was devoted to a soda fountain counter which had twelve swivel stools. During the noon hour there were always lines of school children and neighborhood employees waiting to be served.

The business was begun by Mrs. Finkler's parents, the Kahans. Mr. Finkler worked in the store while he at-
(6) tended high school; after he married the Kahan daughter he was taken into the business. His primary responsibility was to handle the soda fountain. Mr. Kahan died, and Mr. Finkler entered partnership with his mother-in-law, who

5. A sense of meaninglessness is one of the most common aspects of depression.

6. Throughout his adult life, the patient has maintained much the same dependent role he played during adolescence. This seems to be particularly true in his relationship to his mother-in-law, who appears to be the dominant figure in the patient's life.

continued in her role as cashier and bookkeeper. Mrs. Finkler worked in the store part-time.

The Finklers lived above the store until the birth of their second child, at which time Mrs. Kahan bought them a house around the corner, and the Finklers moved into their own home. Mrs. Kahan moved in with them after the death of her husband.

Before his present illness, Mr. Finkler had never suffered from more than an occasional cold, and he hadn't missed more than two days of work in twenty-four years. The income from the business was modest, but according to Mrs. Finkler it was ample enough for their needs.

"What do we want?" she asked Miss Donahue. "We have food in the refrigerator, a roof over our heads, clothes to wear. Maybe," she reflected, "a vacation would be nice, but who has time? In our business, you can't close for holidays."

The family doctor had given Mr. Finkler a thorough physical examination and found nothing wrong. His complaint was fatigue and general depression. Medication was prescribed but was not effective, and Mr. Finkler returned for repeated office visits. Further tests were made and the possibility of physical illness again ruled out. Mr. Finkler remained home while Mrs. Finkler and her mother managed the store.

After several months, Mr. Finkler's condition had not changed, so Mrs. Finkler again consulted the family doctor. He recommended hospitalization and psychotherapy, but Mr. Finkler refused to go to the hospital. One evening, while Mrs. Finkler, her two children, and Mrs. Kahan were in the store, Mr. Finkler attempted to commit suicide by turning on the gas jets. Mrs. Finkler had discovered him when she had gone home on one of her periodic checks to see if he was all right. She insisted that he had never talked about taking his own life. The only reason she had checked on him frequently was that he seemed indifferent to food and she wanted be sure he ate properly. It was after the attempted suicide that Mr. Finkler agreed to be hospitalized.

* * *

When Mr. Finkler reached the psychiatric floor, he asked if he could lie down. He said that he was tired and that his legs felt as though they were caving in. Indeed, his feet dragged, and he had trouble walking. The nurse in charge, Miss Pallin, assigned him a bed, one of four in a small ward room. Mr. Finkler stretched out on the bed and fell asleep until the attendant, Mr. Roberd, awakened him for dinner.

Mr. Roberd tapped Mr. Finkler on the shoulder lightly. "Time to get up for dinner," he said pleasantly. "We don't serve in bed around here."

Mr. Finkler said he was still tired and wasn't hungry. He pleaded to be allowed to stay in bed without eating.

Mr. Roberd thought that Mr. Finkler should get up and insisted that he make an effort. Mr. Finkler struggled to rise.

"How you feeling?" asked Mr. Roberd.

"Not so well," replied Mr. Finkler.

"Anything hurt?" asked Mr. Roberd.

"No," insisted Mr. Finkler. "It's my eyes – they keep shutting."

"Headache?" asked Mr. Roberd.

"No," replied Mr. Finkler. "Will I cause trouble if I don't come to dinner?"

"No," answered Mr. Roberd. "It's your stomach that will be hungry. Maybe some strong black coffee will get you up. Give you some energy. Put in lots of sugar."

Mr. Finkler got up and hunted for his tie. His fingers fumbled, trying to tie a knot, and he gave up.

"You don't need a tie. We're not formal around here."

Mr. Finkler followed Mr. Roberd into the corridor. "I'll show you where you go. Just get a tray, and you can sit anywhere you want to in the dining room," said Mr. Roberd.

The patient line extended into the hallway, and Mr.

Finkler moved back to the end of the line. He leaned against the wall. Other patients got in line behind him, but Mr. Finkler motioned for them to pass him.

Mr. Roberd, who monitored the line to keep it moving, told Mr. Finkler to hold onto his place in the line. "You shouldn't give up your position. Keep moving," he told Mr. Finkler.

"Does it matter?" asked Mr. Finkler.

"Sure it matters," explained Mr. Roberd. "Some of these people will push right ahead. Now you don't have to give your place up. You shouldn't just stand there. The line moves. You keep right up with the line."

"It doesn't matter," said Mr. Finkler quietly. "First or last. It doesn't matter, does it?"

"Why sure it matters. You was there right up front."

"I am sorry," apologized Mr. Finkler.

"There's nothing to be sorry for."

"I didn't mean to mix up the line," said Mr. Finkler. (7)

He was the last to enter the dining room. His plate was filled and he asked for black coffee. Carrying his tray, he looked around the room and went to a rear table where three patients were already seated. He asked their permission to sit down.

"It's a free country," said one patient, a young man in his early twenties. "No assigned places. Grab a place. Dog eat dog."

"If you don't want me to sit here," said Mr. Finkler, "I won't."

"Who said that?"

7. The patient's behaviors reflect a pervasive sense of self-worthlessness. He seems to be apologizing for living. Underlying these manifest expressions of self-worthlessness is often a feeling of guilt, and in working with this patient, it would be important to understand the basis for any possible feelings of guilt.

"I didn't know. I didn't want to bother you." Mr. Finkler took a chair and moved it to the end of the table and placed his tray on his lap.

An attendant, Mr. Martinez, came over and asked Mr. Finkler why he hadn't put his tray on the table. Mr. Finkler became agitated. His hands fumbled and the tray slipped to the floor. Mr. Finkler bent down and tried to scoop the food back onto the plate and pick up the fallen silverware.

"Now why didn't you put your tray on the table? Then this wouldn't have happened."

Mr. Finkler didn't respond. He stacked the plates, cup. and saucer back onto the tray and started to cry. Mr. Martinez offered to get him more food but Mr. Finkler refused. He said he wasn't hungry and didn't feel like eating. He also said he hoped that his not eating wouldn't get him or Mr. Martinez into any trouble.

* * *

Throughout the first week of hospitalization, Mr. Finkler found it impossible to remain awake during the day more than a few hours at a time. He constantly returned to his bed or sat in a corner chair in the day room, drowsing. Miss Borden, a staff nurse, stopped and awakened him one afternoon. She talked about his feelings of fatigue and inability to remain awake.

"Feeling pretty tired, Mr. Finkler?"

He sat up in bed, straightened his jacket and buttoned his shirt collar.

"Tired," he admitted.

"Do you have any idea why you might be tired?"

"No," answered Mr. Finkler. "I thought maybe I was sick. The doctor said I didn't have anything wrong with me."

"You know, Mr. Finkler, sometimes all of us get tired and sleepy when we're bored. I wonder if you might like to get involved in some activities?"

Mr. Finkler shook his head. "What could that do?" he asked.

"Get your mind active, your body active. You'll feel better, Mr. Finkler, when you let yourself get interested in something. Is there some hobby that you have – something in particular that interests you?" (8)

Mr. Finkler sat quietly.

"What did you do, Mr. Finkler? I know you worked."

"A store."

"Would you like to tell me about your store?"

"There's not much to tell," answered Mr. Finkler.

"What kind of store?"

"A little store."

"What did you sell?"

"Different things – you know, magazines, bubble gum, greeting cards – for holidays and birthdays."

"That must have kept you busy."

"It was busy," admitted Mr. Finkler. "Always a customer in and out. A living. I made a living."

"What problems did you have? I imagine a business like yours needs lots of decisions."

"Some," said Mr. Finkler. "Newspapers – I have to get to the store early to get in the newspapers. Maybe there is snow or rain. I have to get the papers in."

"Anything else?"

"Reordering. Like you buy bubble gum; the kids buy the gum; the bubble gum salesman comes; you buy more bubble gum. Then you sell out again. That's the way it goes. Sometimes you reorder and you don't get a delivery. Sometimes you get a delivery and you don't sell. What can I say? Is

8. The psychological dynamics underlying the apparent boredom of a depressed patient may be quite different from those that account for the boredom of a psychologically healthy person. Mechanical involvement in activities may be of little help in such cases; in fact, continued pressure to join activities may increase rather than alleviate the depression.

that right? Am I doing all right?"

"You're doing fine, Mr. Finkler. I take it your business was successful?"

"A living."

"Have you been in business long, Mr. Finkler?"

"Twenty-four years."

"That's a long time."

"A long time," echoed Mr. Finkler.

"Did you start the business?"

Mr. Finkler paused before he answered. "No," he said thoughtfully. "My wife's parents started the business."

"Then you took it over?"

"It wasn't quite like that," said Mr. Finkler. "I married my wife and I worked and then maybe I took over a little bit." He stared out the window. "It's raining," he said to Miss Borden. "When did the rain start?"

"This morning," answered Miss Borden.

"Rain all day. This is the kind of rain you have to get the newspapers in."

"Yes, you said that, Mr. Finkler."

"It was a problem."

"And were you ever worried before, Mr. Finkler?"

"Before what?" he asked, groping for words.

"Before recently."

"I don't know," answered Mr. Finkler. "I think now I don't know. Do we ever know?" he said vaguely. "What do we know? We live; it's not always easy. We go on; we try to go on," said Mr. Finkler. His voice broke, and he started to cry.

"And what, Mr. Finkler?"

"One day."

"Yes, Mr. Finkler?"

"One day you stand and your legs go so." He bent his knees.

"Your legs felt weak?"

"Maybe weak, maybe strong. You don't know. One day you run out of bubble gum."

"And then, Mr. Finkler?" 9

"And that day you look out it is like today with rain, maybe some ice and sleet, and the bubble gum man comes and you don't reorder."

"Did that happen?"

"No," said Mr. Finkler. "I always ordered."

"Did something happen, Mr. Finkler?"

"The ice cream freezer broke down. My wife was sick about it. My mother-in-law thought she would have a heart attack. You have no idea. We had just gotten an ice cream order and the current – I don't know what it was but the motor stopped."

"And what did you do?"

"I laughed." Mr. Finkler turned to Miss Borden. "I laughed. It's only ice cream. So we don't have chocolate. In twenty-four years, we always have chocolate and one day there's no chocolate. I say to myself the world won't fall apart if we don't have chocolate."

"Was everything ruined?"

"Everything. The floor, the freezer, the ice cream, the sherbert – ruined. We could save nothing."

"How did you feel, Mr. Finkler?"

Mr. Finkler paced the room slowly, his chin lowered. He 10
returned to his bed and sat down and burst into tears. "I didn't care," he whispered. "I didn't care. It was ruined, and I didn't care. It was all gone."

9. An almost obsessive concern about an apparently trivial matter, such as the bubble gum, suggests that this topic has some personally significant meaning for the patient that is not obvious to others. One may fail to notice these matters simply because they appear to be trivial; but a seemingly trivial problem may have great psychological meaning for the patient himself.

10. The breakdown of the ice cream freezer obviously has important psychological meaning for Mr. Finkler. His

"What was all gone?"

"Twenty-four years – overnight maybe, all gone. I didn't care."

"Would you like to talk about this feeling, Mr. Finkler?"

"What can I say? There's nothing to say. You're a nice lady. Maybe I bother too much. I talk too much. You have work. Such a job you have here. It's hard work. You like the work?"

Miss Borden said that she wanted to help people and that if Mr. Finkler talked with her she might be able to help him handle his problems.

Mr. Finkler thanked her. He told her how kind she was and he was ashamed and sorry to tell her that it wouldn't do any good to talk. There was nothing she nor anyone else could do.

That wasn't necessarily true, Miss Borden pointed out. Talking about one's problems was important therapeutically.

(11) "Burying a problem," she told him, "isn't a solution. The problem remains. Sometimes we all must face ourselves."

"Why?" asked Mr. Finkler.

statement about his mother-in-law's possible heart attack, his laughter when the breakdown occurred, and his strong emotional reaction upon retelling the story suggest that this incident may involve Mr. Finkler's feelings of hostility and guilt. At this point, this can only be viewed as a tentative hypothesis, and it would be important to explore this issue further. In following this up, however, one must recognize that the incident probably represents a very painful and sensitive area for the patient.

11. Although it is true that self-awareness is a positive therapeutic goal, merely telling a depressed patient that he must face himself is unlikely to be very therapeutic. In fact, making such a statement may have the negative effect of increasing the patient's guilt because he is unable to achieve what is considered the right thing to do.

"Because you want to get better; you want to go back to your family and your work."

"I don't know," said Mr. Finkler quietly.

"You were in your business for a long time," said Miss Borden.

"Twenty-four years – a lifetime, no?"

"That's the point, Mr. Finkler. You don't want to give all this up."

"I don't? Reorder, sell, buy more. So I won't sell chocolate ice cream. Is that bad? The world will go on. My wife and my mother-in-law maybe are better off without me."

"I know that must not be the case."

"How do you know? Did my wife say that?"

"Your life is important and your happiness is important."

"To keep a store open to sell chewing gum? Tell me, nurse, will the world be any different because David Finkler doesn't sell chewing gum?"

* * *

The staff continued their efforts to involve Mr. Finkler in the ward's occupational therapy program. He said he felt clumsy with his hands and hoped no one would mind if he just sat. He told Miss Borden that he had always been on the go, and sitting was a new pleasure for him. He didn't mind not having anything to do. He had never read much; television didn't particularly interest him. He was all right just sitting, unless he was in anybody's way. If that was so, he would sit in the hall or any other place they wanted him to.

Miss Borden explained that he was free to sit and be inactive, but she urged him to become involved for his own benefit. He was encouraged to attend group therapy sessions, which he did, sitting in the back of the room sleeping. Miss Borden rapeatedly encouraged him to enter the group discussions. At one point she asked him to voice his opinion. He rose, shook his head, and openly wept. Some of the other patients felt that he belonged in another group. His depression was contagious. They felt a certain scorn and dislike for Mr. Finkler, who was not embarrassed about weeping. Mr. Finkler told the nurse that he was sorry he had cried but his anxiety about having to talk about how unhappy he was in front of the group had been too painful. He worried that his feelings would upset other people. A few of the patients had told him privately that he made them feel rotten. It upset Mr. Finkler that he was the cause of any trouble.

Miss Borden assured him that he was not any bother and certainly he was welcome to discuss his problems individually if he preferred.

"So I will make *you* feel rotten instead?"

"I won't feel that way."

"I suppose not," said Mr. Finkler.

Although Mr. Finkler was listless and tired during the day, he had difficulty sleeping at night. Late in the evening he would creep into the hall and then sit in a chair in the dayroom until told to return to bed by one of the attendants.

"I can't sleep," he said.

"I'll get a nurse," Mr. Ward told him.

Miss Jackson went in to see Mr. Finkler and asked him what worried him.

"Nothing at all. I just can't sleep."

"You're up all day, and you can't sleep at night?"

"I guess so."

"Any idea why?"

"No."

She gave him a sedative. He thanked her and returned to bed. On the third successive night that he asked for and received a sedative, Mr. Finkler awakened screaming in the middle of the night. He was taken out of the room and brought down to the nurses' station, his body sweating and his speech incoherent.

"What happened? Now let's get a hold of yourself."

Mr. Finkler wrung his hands and wept.

"Now relax; some deep breaths. Let's take this." Miss

Jackson gave him a sedative and a glass of water.

"Feel like talking about what upset you?"

"A nightmare maybe," whispered Mr. Finkler.

"Would you like to describe it?"

"To tell you?" he asked. He panted. "I was running."

"Yes."

"Running. That's all. Running."

"And then?"

"I couldn't stop running. My legs hurt. They felt swollen like lead weights. I tried to stop. I couldn't."

"Was anything making you run?"

Mr. Finkler rocked from side to side. "The ice cream freezer broke, and all the ice cream was ruined." Mr. Finkler (12) started to laugh. "I'm laughing now," he told the nurse. "That's what happened. The ice cream freezer broke and I laughed." He continued to laugh and then said he was ready to go back to bed.

* * *

Whenever Mr. Finkler was asked how he felt, he responded that life was meaningless. "Life has no purpose," he said.

"Twenty-four years," he murmured to Miss Borden. "It's funny I should feel like now all of a sudden I know."

"What do you know?"

"That life is for nothing."

"Your life, Mr. Finkler?"

"What I did – in the store. Every day at six, up to go to

12. Inability to sleep is a symptom, not a cause of Mr. Finkler's problem. In a very real sense, he may be afraid to sleep because he is afraid to dream. Dreaming, of course, involves a certain loss of conscious control, and Mr. Finkler's nightmare suggests that he may be especially afraid about the loss of self-control involved in this incident.

the store and back at eleven. My feet hurt because I stood all day. Do your feet hurt?"

"Sometimes."

"You don't mind?"

"Sometimes I do, of course. But this is something we learn to live with."

"And if you can't?" asked Mr. Finkler.

"Oh, but you can. We all can. Everybody does."

"I am everybody?"

Mr. Finkler's comments and hints about the emptiness of his life concerned the staff. They felt that he might attempt suicide. The staff, alerted to this possibility, became especially observant of his behavior.

One afternoon, Mr. Roberd found him in the medication room. The door had accidentally been left unlocked. Mr. Finkler was looking at the bottles on the shelf and held one in his hand.

"You're not supposed to be in here," Mr. Roberd told him.

"I am sorry," said Mr. Finkler.

"You want to give me that bottle in your hand?"

"Certainly," said Mr. Finkler.

"Did you take anything from that bottle?"

"Of course not," replied Mr. Finkler. "I wondered what kind of medicine the doctor was giving me." He told Mr. Roberd that he didn't know that he was not supposed to go into the room and was terribly sorry. He assured Mr. Roberd that he hadn't disturbed anything.

"Or taken anything?" asked Mr. Roberd.

"God is my witness – nothing," answered Mr. Finkler, turning his pockets inside out.

"I'm not blaming you or accusing you," said Mr. Roberd.

"Nothing. Why should I take something? You think maybe I want to kill myself?"

"You don't want to do nothing like that, Mr. Finkler."

"No, I suppose not," said Mr. Finkler, wandering down the corridor back to his room, where he fell asleep. An hour later, Miss Borden came to rouse him and tell him his wife and mother-in-law had come to visit.

Mrs. Kahan and Mrs. Finkler were seated in the lounge when Mr. Finkler and Miss Borden entered the room. They talked briefly and Miss Borden turned to leave but was detained by Mrs. Kahan.

"Stay. You don't have to run off."

"I can come back. You might want to talk alone first," said Miss Borden.

"What is there to say that you can't hear?" asked Mrs. Kahan. "Tell me, is he better?" (13)

"You can ask Mr. Finkler," said Miss Borden.

"He doesn't look so good," she whispered to Miss Borden before Mr. Finkler answered. "No color. Like a ghost." She turned to Mr. Finkler and asked him how he liked the food.

He said it was all right. "Nothing special."

"You shouldn't worry about food here anyhow," said Mrs. Kahan. "You're in for your head, not your stomach."

Mrs. Kahan asked Miss Borden if the doctor had noticed any change in her son-in-law. Mrs. Finkler interrupted her mother and asked Mr. Finkler if he saw the doctor regularly.

"When he comes," replied Mr. Finkler.

"He doesn't come every day? Why is that?" Mrs. Kahan asked Miss Borden.

"He does see Mr. Finkler several times a week."

"And the rest of the time, what happens? What do you do?" she asked Mr. Finkler.

"Sit and sleep."

"Sit and sleep?" said Mrs. Kahan. "You could do that at home. You don't have to come here to find a place to sleep."

They continued to talk. Mr. Finkler leaned back in the chair and closed his eyes.

13. In some parts of this conversation, Mrs. Kahan seems to act as if Mr. Finkler were not a person. She seems to treat him as an object rather than a person.

"Did he tell you why he is like this?" asked Mrs. Kahan.

"We are discussing his problems," replied Miss Borden.

"He's the last one to have problems," said Mrs. Kahan. "You walked out at the right time, David." She patted her son-in-law's knee. "Are you listening to me, David? Did you know what happened with the freezer? Didn't you tell him?" she asked her daughter. "Do you know what happened with the freezer? Do you know about the freezer?" she said turning to Miss Borden. "We had to get a new one. We tried getting the other one repaired and the money was thrown out. You know why it happened, David? Remember the thermostat? I told you to check the thermostat. You forgot. So the freezer broke. It happens, but you could have said to me, Mom, check the freezer, and so I would have checked. No, you had to do it and this is what happens."

(14) Mr. Finkler began trembling and weeping. Mrs. Finkler and he stood up. He told his wife that he wanted to lie down. She walked back to the room with him.

"He's worse," said Mrs. Kahan to Miss Borden. "I take one look at him – a living death. You think he will get better?"

"I believe he will, Mrs. Kahan, but I suggest that you try not to worry him about the freezer. He is upset enough without your visit making him worse."

"Not worry him? So we have the worries. David shouldn't worry. We do a toe dance around him, so he won't worry. I don't understand, Miss Borden. My husband and I began the store in the depression. Weeks, we didn't eat a crumb. Do you know what it was to work day and night for a penny? Do you know what it was like to wait for a customer, to plead for the bank to wait a day before they took the

14. Here is further evidence of the psychological significance of the freezer incident. Regardless of Mrs. Kahan's intent, her statements unquestionably serve to increase Mr. Finkler's sense of guilt.

store over? It was a living hell, Nurse, a living hell. We make a little bit; we finally get ahead. My husband should have only lived to see what happened to the store – the 15
freezer. Eight hundred dollars for a freezer! Money doesn't grow on trees, Nurse. And you say to me, don't worry David!"

That night Mr. Finkler was unable to sleep. He remained quietly in bed, then rose and paced the halls. Several times he was led back to bed and given a sedative, but he returned to the corridor. Mr. Finkler did not ask for any attention. He pleaded to be allowed to walk in the halls, insisting that he wasn't disturbing anyone. He said that he could not lie in bed because he was too restless. He would walk quietly, he pleaded, but he had to walk.

"What harm is there?" he asked.

"There isn't any harm," said Miss Jackson, "but you should try and get some sleep."

"I can't sleep."

"Is something bothering you?"

Mr. Finkler's answer was a sob and a repetition of his desperate need to walk – to keep walking.

"Are you worried about something, Mr. Finkler?"

He admitted that when he slept he had frightening dreams. The dreams were so real to him, he explained, and they occurred regularly.

"I do not want to dream, and if I sleep this happens," he told her.

"What about your dreams?"

"Nothing," he said. "I don't want to talk about them."

"I think it will help if you do talk about them," insisted Miss Jackson.

"You are torturing me," sobbed Mr. Finkler. "Torturing me. What do you want from me? Blood? What did I do? What do you want from me?" he cried. "I am bothering no one. I stand here. Not a sound. You keep after me. I tell

15. This conversation provides some basis for greater insight into Mrs. Kahan's feelings.

16 you I don't want to talk about them. How many times do I have to beg you?"

"You have to face these things, Mr. Finkler, to get better. You can't repress these feelings."

"I can't," he said. "You will make me? You will force me?" He was sweating profusely and his pajamas were wet with perspiration. Miss Jackson suggested that he change his shirt. He permitted himself to be led back to the room, and he did not get up again that night.

The next day he greeted the staff pleasantly. That day, for the first time since his arrival in the hospital, he remained awake all day. He asked another patient to play a game of checkers. When he saw Mr. Roberd wheeling a cart down the hall, he volunteered assistance.

Miss Borden commented on the striking change in Mr. Finkler. "He's euphoric," she noted. "He's acting like a new staff member. He keeps wanting to know if we need any help."

When he wasn't performing some small chores, he talked to the other patients in the lounge, asking them about themselves and their families. He smiled frequently and occasionally laughed. At mealtimes, he took a place on line and did not step back to allow others to go ahead of him.

That night he told Miss Jackson that he felt much better and assured her that he wouldn't be any trouble. He was sorry for the inconvenience that he had caused the previous night, but he told her he felt very good because he was certain that he had solved the problem of his nightmares.

16. The pain associated with Mr. Finkler's dreams is dramatically shown by his interpretation of the request to talk about the dreams as torture. At this point, comments about the necessity of facing himself are not likely to be very therapeutic.

She told him she was very glad that he had snapped out of his depression.

"That's it," he said snapping his fingers. "No more." He told her he had never felt better in his life, and seemed confident and assured. "I know what I want," he said softly, "It is all clear to me." He was glad that he had talked with her because now he felt completely straightened out and knew that his problems would be resolved.

"You'll see," he told her as he left for bed. "In the morning, a new Mr. Finkler. You'll be surprised, Nurse. They'll all be surprised, my wife, my mother-in-law. She will be happy (17)
and surprised. Maybe you will be here to tell them," said Mr. Finkler. "In the morning. Promise me," he said, as he walked down the hall towards his room.

17. It is apparent that Mr. Finkler has made a decision which has led to a clearcut shift in mood. Whenever a patient shows such a rapid mood swing, regardless of whether it is from depression to euphoria or vice versa, it is important to identify the basis for this change. In this case, sensitivity to Mr. Finkler's changing mood may literally be a matter of life or death.

"OF ALL PEOPLE – NOT DAVID"

1. Tense and anxious, Mr. Finkler is unable to respond to Miss Donahue's questions. How does she react to his resistance? Do you agree with her decision not to continue the intake interview?

2. After Mr. Finkler is taken up to the psychiatric ward, Mrs. Finkler volunteers information about her husband. What does she reveal that might be helpful in understanding Mr. Finkler's anxiety?

3. On the ward, Mr. Finkler complains of fatigue and his inability to get up. The attendant encourages him to go to dinner. How might you explain the meaning of Mr. Finkler's fatigue? What have you done with patients who retreat into sleep and consistently try to escape from activities?

4. Mr. Finkler obediently gets up at Mr. Roberd's request and enters the dining room. Can you offer any interpretations of his behavior on the line and in the dining room? What do his actions reflect about his problem?

5. Miss Borden and Mr. Finkler begin to discuss some of his problems. How well do you feel Miss Borden handled the situation? What does Mr. Finkler reveal about himself? What are his attitudes and perceptions about the kind of life he has led? He dwells on one event – the breakdown of the ice cream freezer. What might this single occurrence have meant to Mr. Finkler?

6. Although Mr. Finkler is inactive during the day, he becomes restless and wakeful at night. What might account for this inversion of night and day? Have you had any experiences with patients who exhibited this same tendency? In what respects did they have problems similar to Mr. Finkler's? Were you able to take any therapeutic action?

7. Mr. Finkler hints at the meaninglessness of his life and the lack of any desire to go on. The staff infer from his comments that he is potentially suicidal and should be closely observed. Do you feel they were right in making this assumption? What are the bases for your opinions?

8. The possibility of a patient taking his own life is a significant concern for the staff of any mental hospital. In your experience, what staff measures are customarily taken when patients pose this kind of threat? What might you have done in the case of Mr. Finkler?

9. Miss Borden is present when Mr. Finkler's wife and mother-in-law come to visit. Describe the interactions which take place. Should Miss Borden have intervened more than she did? Describe Mrs. Kahan's most likely reaction to her conversation with Miss Borden.

10. After the departure of his family, Mr. Finkler is unable to sleep, and Miss Jackson presses him to talk about his problems. Mr. Finkler resists and accuses Miss Jackson of torturing him. Are there any other approaches Miss Jackson might have used to allay Mr. Finkler's fears? Miss Jackson maintains that talking about one's problems helps. Do you feel this is true in the case of Mr. Finkler after his family's visit?

11. Mr. Finkler displays a striking behavioral change. Does his dramatic swing of mood suggest anything to you? What interpretations can you offer? What would you do if you were working with Mr. Finkler?

5

The Trial

Maria Sanchez was accused of immoral conduct. Three patients who shared Maria's four-bed ward room went together to the nurses' station to report her behavior. The head nurse, Mrs. Lyle, encouraged them to discuss the charge, but the women refused to speak with her, insisting they would only talk to Miss Moller, a floor nurse whose sympathetic understanding they felt they could rely on.

"She's the one nurse around here who listens. You can take the rest and dump them. They tell you something and then they go around behind your back and get an order to give you a needle," said the leader of the group, Miss Kanter. Her heavy-set figure was emphasized by a long, flowing dressing gown.

Miss Moller was called to the nurses' station and escorted the three women to an office where she assured them they could discuss their feelings in complete privacy. She offered them cigarettes.

"I've never been here before," said Miss Kanter, looking around at the desks and file cabinets.

"This is a working office for the staff," explained Miss Moller.

"Is the door locked?"

"I can lock the door." Miss Moller locked the door and the women relaxed.

Miss Moller asked them to tell her what had happened.

"We couldn't sleep, could we, dearies?" said Miss Kanter. The other women nodded their heads in agreement.

"And now we have splitting headaches – all of us." The other patients again nodded their heads, concurring with Miss Kanter's report of their physical discomforts.

"I've been here for four months, and let me tell you nothing like this has ever happened. It just goes to prove that the people in here are sane and the ones outside are nutty. Then Maria Sanchez came."

"When did she come?" asked Miss Moller. "She's a new patient. I don't know her. I was off yesterday."

"She came last night – late last night," explained Mrs. Torrence.

"She came after supper," Miss Kanter contradicted.

"Yes, after supper." Mrs. Torrence, a fragile woman, brushed strands of red-gold and white hairs from her bloodshot eyes. "See my eyes," she said. "They're tearing. I didn't sleep last night."

"She was put in our room," the third patient, Miss Ocher, began timidly. "I was nice. You know how I'm nice," she said to Miss Moller. "I know how it is when you come to a place like this and right off you're lonely. I showed her where the toilet and showers were; I told her she must *not* put paper towels in the toilet. She showed what she was like. I tried to tell her what paper towels did to toilets only to have her scream at me that she never used paper towels when she went to the toilet."

"You didn't tell us she yelled at you," said Mrs. Torrence. "I didn't talk much to her." She leaned over to retie the laces of her sneaker. "I'm not one to judge her just because she has a temper. I'm angry because of the perfume that she sprayed. She said our room was stinking from antiseptics. I told her we didn't like the smell of that perfume; she asked me if I liked 'stink' better."

Miss Moller interrupted the individual accounts of Maria's disturbing behavior.

"I can see that you're upset by the way she talked to you when you were all trying to be helpful, but there's a big difference between her saying that she didn't use paper towels or didn't like the room smelling of antiseptics and saying that she is *immoral.*"

"That isn't all. Do you think we would complain about that?" Miss Kanter angrily stamped out the cigarette and asked Miss Moller if she could borrow another. She would pay Miss Moller back later in the day.

"What she did later is what really upset us," explained Miss Kanter.

"What did she do?" Miss Moller asked. "She must have done something or you ladies wouldn't be so upset. What *did* she do in the room last night? Did she try to approach you, for example?"

"What do you mean, approach?" asked Miss Kanter. "She wouldn't dare. I'd sue the hospital. I've had them outside – not women, but men following me around, and when you're not looking, they sneak up. Before you know it they've had you."

Miss Ocher interrupted. "I'll tell you what she did. I was there when it started. You ladies were brushing your teeth. She got undressed for bed. She was getting undressed when you came back. Remember?"

"That seems reasonable," said Miss Moller.

"She got undressed and that," said Miss Ocher, sitting stiffly upright in the chair, "is exactly where she stopped." She inhaled her cigarette deeply.

Miss Moller said, "Yes?"

"What do you mean, yes?" asked Miss Ocher.

"Maria got undressed and stopped," repeated Miss Moller.

"But that's the point," Miss Kanter argued. "She had nothing on, not a stitch. She stood in the middle of the room. The door was open. She was all exposed, and she kept using a hand mirror to look at herself all over. I put out the light and closed the door. She put on the light and opened the door. We told her it was indecent to be standing like that looking at herself and that it was God's will to wear a nightie to bed like a lady."

"And then," interrupted Miss Ocher breathlessly, "she called the three of us damn fools and said we were to mind our own damn business. She said other things but I can't say them. It was so foul, what came out of her mouth – straight from the gutter."

Because of the tension they showed by their restless movements and tears, Miss Moller suggested the women not continue the conversation at this time, but relax, get some morning coffee, and watch television. She would check into the matter and would certainly speak to them later about what action might be taken.

The women all felt they could not return to the room until Maria was removed. "She's in there now. She didn't get up for breakfast and she said to hell with rules," added Miss Kanter.

Although the women were eager to continue talking about what had happened, Miss Moller insisted they not discuss the (1) matter any longer but wait until she had spoken with Maria.

"Don't let her fool you. That's the kind that can be sweet and then put a knife in your back," warned Miss Kanter.

The hospital consisted of two sections, a new building and adjoining older wings that were scheduled for eventual demolition. However, plans to tear down the older sections

1. Having heard the nature of the complaint, Miss Moller seems eager to stop the conversation, presumably because of the apparent tension shown by the patients. It is perhaps true that continuing to focus on their complaints about Maria may have led to increased tension, but merely blocking discussion can hardly be expected to resolve the tension automatically.

had been repeatedly delayed for several years because of a curtailment of funds and the need for bed space. Although the older units were in full use, only a minimum of plumbing and wiring repairs, sufficient to satisfy building codes, had been carried out. Because the new structure surrounded the older building on three sides, corridors, balconies, and even some patient windows had been blocked by the new building's walls and air shafts.

The psychiatric floors were dark. There was no cross-ventilation. Soot-covered blades from ancient ceiling fans did nothing more than circulate stiffly the trapped summer heat. Maria's room, located in the middle of the corridor, was intended for two patients, but conditions made it necessary to have four beds in the room. These filled nearly all the available floor space.

When Miss Moller opened the door, Maria, a tall, muscular, attractive thirty-eight-year-old woman, was nude, stretched out on the bed in a relaxed position. Her arms were flung out to either side, and the sheet was crumpled on the floor. Miss Moller picked up the sheet and covered Maria, which awakened her.

Startled, she punched off the sheet and sat up in bed. With one hand she twisted her long hair, coiling it in place on top of her head.

(2) "It's late," said Miss Moller. "You've missed breakfast."

2. It would seem that Miss Moller too is discomfited by Maria's nudity. On the one hand, it would be important to understand the motivation of Maria's behavior, but on the other hand, it would also be important to understand why Maria's behavior makes others so uncomfortable. Note also that Miss Moller's first remark to Maria is something of a reprimand, and this influences the emotional tone of their subsequent interactions. Having initiated the relationship in a reprimanding, controlling role, it will probably be more difficult for Miss Moller to shift to an understanding, therapeutic role in her work with Maria.

"Who are you?"

"I'm Miss Moller. I've come on duty this morning, and I understand you arrived last evening."

"I'm Maria Sanchez."

"You missed breakfast, "said Miss Moller, picking up the sheet again and draping it around Maria.

"I'm not hungry. Only an idiot could eat in this heat."

"You must get up for meals," said Miss Moller.

"If I'm not hungry, I have to eat? What kind of crazy rule is that?"

"It's not a crazy rule," explained Miss Moller. "We have many patients here. We have regular meal times. There isn't food available between meals. Just think how hungry you're going to be when lunchtime comes."

"I like to feel hungry."

"You'll be miserable. It's a long time between dinner and lunch the next day."

"Is that why you got me up? To tell me I'm hungry?" Maria groaned and flung herself back on the bed and closed her eyes.

"Now let's keep the sheet up," said Miss Moller. "Have you a dressing gown or a robe? We'll have to get your clothes unpacked. I'm sure you must have a robe." Miss Moller searched a mound of silk dresses and shoes which were in a heap next to Maria's bed.

"I do not have a robe," said Maria.

"Oh now, you *must* have a nightgown and robe. You have 3
so many lovely dresses and all these shoes. What color is your nightgown?"

"Never in my life have I bought a nightgown."

3. It is almost as if Miss Moller doesn't hear the patient, as if not having a nightgown is too far removed from her expectations to register as meaningful information. Thus, the initial conflict is further complicated by a lack of communication.

"Something like this, is this your nightgown?"

"That is my dress."

"It would make a lovely nightgown."

"You want me to wear a good dress for a nightgown – to go to bed?" Maria raised her arms in astonishment.

"Well then, we can find something in the hospital for you to wear."

"Why?"

"At night, Maria. You wear a nightgown at night."

"I do not wear clothes at night. Never! When the sun goes down in the summer I take off my clothes."

"It's *not* what we do here at the hospital."

"In this heat?" asked Maria. "I would choke to death." She grasped her throat and squeezed it. "I could not breathe. I would go mad. I would suffocate." She pulled at her hair. "Look, I can squeeze water from my hair. And here," she stroked her body, "wet everywhere."

"A gown won't make you all that much hotter. It will even be cooler. Just a light gown."

"I do not believe that. I would like to take off my skin in such heat. A gown would stick here and here." Maria pounded various parts of her body. "Why do you want me to wear a gown?" she asked, swinging her legs over the side of the bed and standing up. "You think it is bad to show my body? It's not bad," she argued. "Maybe here a bit too much." She pinched her thigh and said, "I must exercise. I do not like this extra padding."

"The fact is, Maria, there are other patients in the room. One of the important lessons to learn in the hospital is to
(4) respect other patients. They have feelings just as you have feelings and we try and appreciate other people's feelings. It's a first step towards getting well – getting better."

4. Relatively abstract discussions about respect for others are rarely effective in achieving concrete behavior change in a situation such as this.

"You mean," asked Maria, "that if I wear a nightgown you will send me home? I get better just like that?" She snapped her fingers. 'The doctor said it would take time. He wouldn't tell me how long. Now you tell me all I have to do is wear a nightgown and that's the end of my problems."

"I didn't say that. I said that it *is* important for you to consider the feelings of other patients. These women in the room here have feelings. You have to try and understand how they feel and they have to understand how you feel."

"So that's it," said Maria. She knotted the sheet and threw it towards Miss Moller.

"The others you believe. Their feelings you like. Let me tell you how I feel. Last night I come. It's hell in here. No wind. The air like a noose on my neck. I sweat like an animal. Then we are told to go to bed. Thank God. I take off my clothes. My god, my dress like a dish rag. I could scratch sweat from my back in a pool. And what do those women do? That one," she said, directing a finger toward a bed opposite hers, "that one with the hair in colors like I never saw in my life. She puts on two nightgowns and then wears slipper socks to bed. And the fat one who talks like she has a megaphone – it bursts my ear drums – she climbs under a blanket and I see her moving around and I watch. She comes out in ten, maybe fifteen minutes with a robe buttoned up to here," Maria pointed to her chin, "and on her head she has a scarf. And then I look. I think I have seen everything but the other one doesn't even get undressed. She has a girdle, bra, a dress, and a sweater and she climbs under the sheet. I think of the sweat rolling down their bodies. I cannot stand it. I say to myself, Maria, be nice. These women are crazy or they wouldn't be here. I am crazy but not like that. I have to help them. I show them how good it feels to have no clothes. I show them they do not have to go to bed like they are going out into a snowstorm. It's summer. We have a heat wave. I ask my doctor. He comes today. I say to him, I am in a crazy place. I ask him what he wears to bed at night in a hot room that has no air-conditioning and has three other people sweating."

5 "We're *going* to get dressed now, aren't we, Maria? You're *not* going to throw sheets at me. You can talk to your doctor later. We'll talk about what you must wear at night. Here, why not put on this nice dress?"

"I wonder," said Maria, walking over and facing Miss Moller. "You maybe do not like naked people? I could understand if you were ugly and old. But you are a pretty girl. You have a nice figure. OK, I see, maybe some naked people make you sick. I do not like those either. They have too much in the wrong place. But me, like you – I too have a nice body."

"We'll just go ahead and put on this dress, and I'll see that you get some coffee and toast. We usually don't do that. We expect our patients to be up on time for meals. But I'm sure we can make an exception this time."

"I told you, I'm not hungry. I stay here and sleep naked, or I go out into the hall like I am." She started to walk toward the open door. Miss Moller blocked her and shut the door.

"You are going to listen, aren't you, Maria? You're *not* going to walk out into the hall without clothes. You are going to wear a nightie to bed. You're *not* going to scream at the
6 nurses like this. If you don't follow the rules, I do think we will have to place you in seclusion. We simply cannot have a patient doing exactly as she wishes. There are other people around here to consider."

5. Apparently at the end of her patience, Miss Moller relies on repetition to achieve her immediate goal. The interaction between nurse and patient started with a reprimand, and now seems to have deteriorated into a conflict in which the chances of reaching some understanding are growing even slimmer.

6. Having failed to resolve the conflict, Miss Moller resorts

"Seclusion?" asked Maria. "What's that?" She pounded the pillow with her fists.

"If you can't get along with other people, you'll have to be put where you are alone and you will only have yourself to disturb."

Miss Moller opened the door and summoned an aide whom she told to remain with Maria to prevent her from leaving the room.

Miss Moller returned to the nurses' station and checked Maria's record regarding ordered medication for sedation. Concealing the medication in her uniform pocket, Miss Moller returned to the room. The aide reported that during Miss Moller's absence, Maria had not moved from her bed. The aide had busied herself folding Marie's clothing and commenting on the attractiveness of the various dresses. "She has a fortune in clothes," said the aide. "If I was her," she told Miss Moller, "you wouldn't find me sitting around in my bare bottom. I'd be glad to wear any of these dresses."

The aide was asked to hold Maria's arm while Miss Moller administered a sedating intramuscular injection. Maria (7) struggled, protesting that they were treating her like a prisoner. "I don't want no drugs," she screamed. "I'll come out of here a junkie. You're making me a junkie."

Miss Moller patted Maria's arm. "We're not doing anything of the sort. I've just given you something to help you be quiet. You're upset. It's a new place. Now let's get dressed. You're going to be a good girl and I'll see that you not only get coffee and toast, but how about some orange juice? We could get some orange juice, couldn't we?" Miss Moller asked the aide.

Although voicing strong objections, Maria did not physi-

to threat, and the emotional intensity of their interaction mounts.

7. One wonders, of course, if the patient has been sedated primarily because the nurse is upset.

cally resist when Miss Moller and the aide dressed her. She complained, "I'll tell my doctor I've got to get the hell out of this prison."

"We're not a prison," said Miss Moller. "We're here to help you. Would you like to go down to the patient lounge?"

Escorted by the aide and Miss Moller, Maria was brought down to the crowded patient lounge. Miss Moller instructed the aide to remain with Maria for a while to make certain that she would behave quietly. After Miss Moller returned to the nurses' station, Maria launched into an abusive account of Miss Moller's brutality. Other patients clustered around to hear the report, sympathetically shaking their heads and adding stories of their own regarding ill treatment. One patient told Maria, "That's what you'll get around here. You learn quick. Do what you're told and you're fine. Break some rule and they get you. I've learned to keep my mouth shut."

Maria said that she had never kept her mouth shut and certainly wasn't going to start now.

One of the patients, Mr. Scott, a man in his early fifties, told Maria that he was upset about what had happened and was particularly surprised that Miss Moller had behaved in such a way. Mr. Scott told Maria that he had been a patient for twenty years. "Years ago you were treated like an animal. It's different now. Twenty years ago you were tied up and you could stay tied up. Now look at me. I have all sorts of privileges." He told Maria that there were "all kinds" on the staff. He was disturbed, however, to hear that Miss Moller had become tough like Mrs. Lyle. "It's a good idea to stay out of Mrs. Lyle's way," he warned Maria, "but Miss Moller is very nice." Several other patients agreed that Miss Moller usually was quite sympathetic.

The aide intervened and told Mr. Scott and the other patients to stop telling stories to Maria and getting her worked up. "You got no business," she told Maria, "running around without clothes. I'm not saying that what you done was wrong, and I'm not saying what she done was right, but you got to wear clothes and that's a rule. Now why don't you all watch television or go down to O.T. and make yourself something?" She got up, turned up the volume of the television and returned to the nurses' station.

After the aide left the room, Mr. Scott told Maria, "You don't have to take it from the nurse or the aides." A patient, he explained, had rights, and he suggested that all the patients should know what had happened. As president of the patient group, he felt that this was just the sort of problem to be discussed at a ward meeting. One was scheduled for the next afternoon, and Mr. Scott said that he would start discussing the matter with the patients and present the case at the meeting.

Maria was quiet all that afternoon and evening. Miss Moller went off duty at five. That evening Maria again undressed and the three patients complained to the attending staff. The immediate solution suggested by an aide was to place a screen around Maria's bed. The patients were told that the matter would be handled the following day.

The next morning Maria was seen by Dr. Wood, and immediately after that he asked Miss Moller and Mrs. Lyle into his office to discuss the situation. He explained that he had just talked with Maria, who was extremely upset and had complained about the staff's treatment of her. Miss Moller defended her actions. She reported that the previous morning she had entered Maria's room after other patients had complained about her immoral behavior. Maria was sleeping without any covering or clothing. When Miss Moller had awakened her, Maria had become abusive, thrown a sheet at Miss Moller, and had made a number of insulting and suggestive remarks. Miss Moller felt that Maria was the kind of patient who could be handled only by immediately establishing authority. "Without limits," she noted, "we cannot function. It isn't just a one nurse to one patient situation. We cannot have the patients doing whatever they want to without consideration of others, and we can't have them running around without clothes!" Is was her belief that limits must start from the first minute of arrival; otherwise an entire floor could be disrupted and the result would be bedlam.

"It isn't the first time we've had patients who wouldn't wear clothes. We have to use seclusion." Miss Moller said that the threat of seclusion had worked in Maria's case because she had agreed to dress and had remained dressed throughout that day. She reminded Dr. Wood that he himself had ordered seclusion for another of his female patients who had behaved in a similar way the previous month.

Dr. Wood replied that the pathology of the two cases
(8) was completely different. In the other case, the symptom could only have been handled with isolation. "Furthermore," he noted, "the other patient had exposed herself in public places, the lounge and on the grounds. Maria's exhibitionism, and I hesitate to use this word to describe Maria's action, was confined to a hot room on a particularly humid night. Maria has a long history of depression and alcoholism, but not of exhibitionism."

He explained that Maria Sanchez was the daughter of a Portuguese sponge fisherman who had been absent from home for long periods of time. Reared by a maternal grandmother – her mother had died when Maria was an infant – she was a talented, self-trained singer and dancer who eventually found her way to the United States as a member of an ethnic dancing group. When the other dancers returned to Portugal, Maria remained, supporting herself as a singer,

8. With others now involved in the conflict, issues have become broader and more diffuse. Added to the initial discomfort at the beginning of the conflict are matters as large as reactions to authority and the need for limits. Meanwhile, no one has been particularly concerned with understanding either Maria or the patients who complained about her behavior.

dancer, and waitress. Over the years she lived with a number of men, liaisons which never became lasting. The last man was much younger than Maria. A year before her commitment, he had walked out on her, accusing her of becoming an "old woman" whom he had never loved but merely used. This led Maria to excessive drinking and recurrent periods of depression. Unable to work steadily and to support herself, she drank more heavily and became more despondent.

Maria was alone. Her father had died; the grandmother was no longer living. Relatives were scattered in Spain and Portugal, and Maria could not recall either their names or addresses.

Thus, in Maria's case, Dr. Wood pointed out, the threat of seclusion held particular terrors. Indeed, any sug- 9
gestion of this nature could possibly motivate Maria to other exaggerated actions. Maria should not be isolated or threatened with isolation. He suggested that she be moved into another room with more compatible roommates.

Mrs. Lyle said this was impossible at the moment. All beds were filled. In the present room arrangement, patients had been cooperating beautifully. "It is unfair to disrupt other patients to help Maria." She would, however, do her best as soon as a bed became available. Since several patients were scheduled to be discharged at the end of the week, a readjustment of roommates was a possibility.

Doctor Wood felt that it would be in Maria's best interest if all similar behavior on her part was ignored without comment. "It is my guess that she will use this undressing to manipulate only if she gets a reaction. Furthermore, as long as she only does this at night, there isn't any cause for real concern."

9. Dr. Wood has more or less assumed the role of Maria's defense attorney, rather than focusing on the interactions that have occurred and helping the staff understand how the sequence of events was leading to a rapidly growing crisis.

Miss Moller said she would follow his suggestion but the problem really hadn't ended, and she told him about the ward meeting scheduled for that afternoon. Maria had told all the patients about what Miss Moller had done to her. Many of the patients were very upset and Mr. Scott, the president of the group, had told Miss Moller they were going to go over what had happened in great detail. The staff generally did not interfere in the topics selected for ward discussions. But in this case, Miss Moller felt that she was being tried. She was quite disturbed about the patients' discussions, reports of which had been brought back to her by the aides who had heard various scattered conversations.

"I think it would be helpful, Dr. Wood, if you could come to the meeting. I wonder if the meeting should be cancelled until a later time when everything would be forgotten."

Dr. Wood regretted not being able to attend. Unfortunately, he was scheduled for an afternoon conference, but he said the staff should go and avoid becoming involved.
(10) "It won't hurt to let them talk the problem out. I don't think this meeting should be cancelled."

The discussion between Dr. Wood, Miss Moller, and Mrs. Lyle was abruptly ended when Dr. Wood was called to the telephone. He told them that he would like to be kept informed, and there would be an opportunity for him to go over the details of Maria's case later in the week or at the beginning of the next week. As he left the room to answer the call, he commented, "Drop the clothes

10. Although patient involvement in the governance of a ward can often have significant therapeutic value, it is unreasonable to expect that merely talking about the problem at a general ward meeting will inevitably solve the conflict. Dr. Wood might have played a more effective role by immediately and directly dealing with the patients involved, and attempting to help the staff gain greater insight into the interaction process that occurred.

issue. Remember it's only at night. And it was a hot night. She'll think differently when the weather turns cold. I think she can be reasoned with. Take it easy at the meeting and don't feel threatened." (11)

After Dr. Wood left, Mrs. Lyle told Miss Moller that she was overreacting to the aides' reports and certainly she shouldn't attend to the comments of Mr. Scott and the other patients. "You must not take a patient's word for what will happen at that meeting. They are always talking about what they are going to do. By the time the meeting comes, many of them will have forgotten about what the staff did, and you can intervene and tell them that Dr. Wood *knows all about the matter* and he *will* handle it! Suggest they start talking about some other subject."

"Won't you be there?"

"I have an administrators' meeting about new case record forms," replied Mrs. Lyle. "Administration decided that all Y-2 forms are going to be kept in the downstairs office and we will have a duplicate form to keep on the floor. I can't say that I'm pleased about this. This means double work and day-to-day entries in triplicate." She discussed the complications of the variety of forms and told Miss Moller that she would explain the new procedures at the staff meeting the following morning. "I think I'll keep the forms in the same file with our present floor records."

At three-thirty the patients began drifting into the lounge for the floor meeting. Miss Moller searched for the other two staff nurses, but one had left early and the other had taken a late coffee break. The psychologist was occupied with a diagnostic work-up of a new patient. Thus the only staff present other then Miss Moller were a dance therapist and a social worker who whispered to Miss Moller that he

11. But of course Miss Moller *does* feel threatened, and telling her not to feel threatened is unlikely to be very helpful.

could only remain for the first part of the meeting because he had an appointment with the family of a patient scheduled for discharge.

Mr. Scott waited until all the patients arrived before calling the meeting to order. The first topic to be discussed was one held over from the previous meeting concerning the failure of patients to assume responsibility for cleaning assignments. In particular, patients of Ward B had not been attending to routine household chores with any regularity; floors were not swept; towels were not distributed; on several occasions no toilet paper had been placed in the bathrooms. A schedule was posted, but patients had neglected to do the various jobs.

"The place is filthy," complained an elderly woman who was in charge of the household lists for the week. "I been a maid lots of places. I seen them all. This place and the places where I worked, cigarette butts got to go in ashtrays. That goes for outside and in here too. We got no business letting people take their butts and throw them on the floor. We got to stop this."

The social worker left during the active discussion
(12) regarding the lack of cleanliness of that particular ward; the dance therapist told Miss Moller that she also had to leave early. Miss Moller remained as the only attending staff member.

After extracting promises from the ward B patients to pay more attention to household matters, Mr. Scott announced that one of the other patients had a very special problem to bring up for discussion. Maria was asked to

12. Dr. Woods is busy; Mrs. Lyle is engaged in administrative matters; the psychologist, social worker, and dance therapist have other duties. Thus, Miss Moller is left alone in a very difficult situation, with little realistic guidance from her supervisor or the responsible physician, and no support from other members of the staff.

stand and introduce herself. Mr. Scott asked the patients to be quiet and to listen. Maria walked up to the front of the room, stood next to Mr. Scott and quietly began her report regarding "abuse" by one of the nurses. She did not mention Miss Moller; however, many of the patients at that point turned and looked over at Miss Moller, who was seated near the door of the room.

"I came here to be helped like all of you." Maria spoke persuasively. "I was insulted." She described how this certain nurse whom she didn't want to mention by name had come into her room, accused her of all sorts of behavior and then finally had given her an injection "for her nerves." Maria said that she had been miserable and afraid to do anything. She didn't know how to contact her doctor. She didn't know what would happen to her. She was terrified, particularly after a suggestion had been made to her about far worse things happening to her if she didn't calm down.

"She's a liar," shouted Miss Torrence.

"She didn't wear no clothes," called Miss Ocher.

"They bring all kinds in here from the streets," said Miss Kanter.

Mr. Scott banged his fist on the table, demanding silence. Some of the patients began talking among themselves, but Maria continued her condemnation of the nurse and the ill-treatment she had endured.

Finally Miss Moller stood up and told Mr. Scott that the subject being discussed was inappropriate and that further discussion should be deferred until Dr. Wood was consulted.

"Why can't we talk about it?" argued Mr. Scott. He told Miss Moller that he could see no reason for maintaining silence. The purpose of the floor meeting was to explore problems concerning the patients. He felt that the dissatisfaction Maria was expressing was a most appropriate topic for discussion.

When Miss Moller again tried to shift the topic, Maria screamed, "You're scared of the truth. You're not going to push me around. You remember that!"

Other patients agreed and said that it was about time they had a chance to tell the truth about what happened to them in this hospital. Other complaints about staff behavior were cited. Mr. Scott demanded order, but the patients continued talking. Maria remained standing next to Mr. Scott. During a lull in the conversation, Maria repeated her story.

Miss Moller went out into the corridor, located several of the aides, and asked them to help her restore order. Patients were directed back to their rooms, to the occupational therapy room, or to various activities.

When Mrs. Lyle returned to the floor, aides and several distraught patients reported what had happened. They could not understand why Miss Moller had broken up the meeting. They were suppossed to have floor government. Problems were to be discussed. Maria Sanchez had introduced a relevant problem and the response of Miss Moller had been to forbid all discussion. When Miss Moller came on duty the next day, Mrs. Lyle confronted her with the report. She reminded Miss Moller that Dr. Wood had expressly said that patients must be given the opportunity to explore their feelings. "It would have been much wiser on your part if you had just stayed there and let them all talk out their feelings. You don't adjourn a meeting just because someone is upset or a patient sounds angry. I'm sorry," she added," that I wasn't there."

Miss Moller defended her action, saying that she had no other alternative but to stop the meeting. Patients were agitated. "They were all talking at once. Mr. Scott could not maintain order, and I tried but at that point you couldn't get any of them to listen. Maria had them stirred up to such a point that if I hadn't stepped in we would have had serious trouble."

"I think you have a problem with Maria," said Mrs. Lyle. "You must remember she is a patient."

"I know she's a patient," answered Miss Moller, "but that doesn't mean there aren't limits. She threw that sheet at me.

I'm lucky that's all she had in her hand. I was angry. I bet you would be angry, too. I stood there and told her she had to wear clothes. If I hadn't stopped her she would have walked in the hall without clothes. I know the other patients. None of them would have started up at that meeting if it hadn't been for Maria. And I can't understand Mr. Scott. We could always depend on him. I have a feeling we had better watch those two. You wouldn't have recognized Mr. Scott. He seemed to be enjoying himself. None of this would have happened except for her. And how could I get her out of there?"

Miss Moller was very disturbed about the meeting, feeling that she had been put in an extremely awkward position without the support of other staff members. The meeting had gone out of control. "The patients were not in any mood to listen to reason. You couldn't stop Maria. She was having her day. Since when," she asked Mrs. Lyle, "do patients run the ward and put the staff on trial? They didn't only blame me but they started complaining about other staff members. Some of them resent being here and who else do they have to blame but the staff? Under the circumstances," she asked Mrs. Lyle, "what could I possibly have done?" (13)

13. One can legitimately sympathize with Miss Moller and emphathize with her feelings about being on trial. But is is also important to recognize the process leading to her extraordinarily difficult position, a process to which she as well as the patients and other staff members contributed. Little or no attention was paid to the motivations of the individuals involved or the interactions between individuals, and thus, without adequate understanding, appropriate and effective steps in intervention were not taken.

THE TRIAL

1. Miss Moller, a staff nurse, encourages a delegation of patients to talk about their negative feelings about another patient. What purpose can this serve? What negative effects might this have? The patients making the charges are seen in a group. Would you have seen the patients individually or together? What effects might the group have had on each other's reactions?

2. Miss Moller acknowledges the negative feelings expressed and does not pass judgment or evaluate the events. Would you have behaved differently?

3. After speaking to the group, Miss Moller goes in to see Maria. Her first reaction is to cover Maria with a sheet, after which she criticizes her for having failed to get up on schedule. Do you feel the patients' complaints about Maria influenced Miss Moller's attitudes towards Maria? Have you ever found yourself influenced or predisposed toward a patient because of other peoples' chance remarks or attitudes? How was your behavior affected?

4. The patient's complaints largely focused on modesty. Do you feel Miss Moller overreacts to this concern?

5. In talking to Maria, Miss Moller stresses the need for her to respect others. Awareness of other people's feelings and reactions is a step towards getting well, she tells Maria. Maria denies that she has been indifferent and presents her version of what occurred. She feels that the other patients are not trying to see how she feels. How do you feel about this question? Would you agree? How might Maria interpret the criticism of her behavior by Miss Moller or the other patients?

6. Miss Moller insists that Maria must put on clothes. She stubbornly resists and Miss Moller threatens seclusion unless Maria complies. Discuss the use of punitive actions

or threats such as restraints or seclusion on controlling patient behaviors.

7. Miss Moller administers the sedative intramuscularly. Why might she have chosen this method rather than permit Maria to take the medication orally?

8. Frequently, staff members employ terms such as "good girl" – "good boy" when addressing patients. Why might these phrases be used? What effect do these phrases have on defining the roles of staff members and patients?

9. The aide directly intervenes in the patient discussion. Do you agree with her direct approach? Do you feel that she should have remained with the patients instead of leaving? Would her presence have short-circuited the subsequent development of personal animosities on Maria's part?

10. Miss Moller feels limits must be established immediately with Maria. To what extent might limits be necessary and realistic in psychiatric wards?

11. Dr. Wood feels that Maria's exposure of her body has a different motivation than purposeful exhibitionism. Do you concur with his analysis? Should he have provided the staff with more information regarding Maria's background? To what extent has lack of communication affected the staff's relationship with the patient?

12. Dr. Wood suggests that the staff ignore Maria's undressing. Tolerating idiosyncratic patient behavior in a ward situation poses problems. How can this problem be handled? Can you cite instances from your past experience where toleration of an individual's behavior resulted in disruption of others? What was done, if anything, to relieve the situation? What suggestions can you offer to help alleviate this problem?

13. Miss Moller feels threatened by the patient group meeting. She is the only staff member left at the meeting,

since the other members have commitments which prevent their attending. What are your feelings about matter? In addition to being aware of patient needs, to what extent do you feel staff members should counsel and support each other?

14. Miss Moller stops the patient group meeting from proceeding. Do you agree with her decision? Why was she uncomfortable in the situation? Was she realistic in perceiving the meeting and discussions as a personal attack?

15. In discussing the events with Mrs. Lyle, Miss Moller concedes that she felt angry. Can you recall instances where you have felt anger toward a patient? Should staff members be able to express their anger to patients? Have you ever expressed your anger to a patient? What occurred? Can you review the dynamics of the situation and describe how you felt?

16. Emotions naturally play an important part in any interaction between people. What special problems may arise in psychiatric situations?

6

"Where Did You Grow Up?"

Luis Rodriguez appeared regularly for his scheduled appointments at the store-front community mental health clinic. Although he came on time, he resisted the therapist's attempts to discuss his problems. He sat slumped in a chair during all of the forty-five minute sessions. Long hair fell to his shoulders, and his eyes remained partially closed as he concentrated on playing an elaborately decorated guitar.

At the close of the fourth session, Miss Lawson, a psychiatric nurse, pointedly asked him why he bothered to come if he didn't want to talk about his problems. Mr. Rodriguez responded by playing a number of chords and then replied, "Why the hell do we do anything in life?"

"We do things for different reasons. I assume you came here because you wanted help."

"Are you serious?"

"Yes, I am serious."

"Kid, you have lots to learn. Time, what's time? Talk, what's talk? What the hell does talking get you in life?"

"Through talking we can resolve problems, or at least try to."

"Where did you grow up?"

"In the city, Mr. Rodriguez."

"Baby, so did I." Mr. Rodriguez leaned over and patted Miss Lawson on the knee. "But, baby, I got a feeling that you and me sat on different front stoops."

"May I ask why you are coming?"

"You mean you don't know? The police, baby. The police. This is going to help me, they said. I need therapy. I need to get adjusted. I need to find myself. Twenty-nine, and I got to find myself. Baby, there are times when I know who I am. There are times when I knew exactly what it means to be Luis Rodriguez. Those times are in my mind, baby. You don't forget those times."

"Why don't you tell me about them."

Mr. Rodriguez stopped playing his guitar and laughed. "You're serious?" he said. "You really mean that?"

"Certainly, I mean that."

"You won't corner me. You think I want a second charge against me? I want to be free, baby, free."

"I can't see how telling me about those times you truly felt yourself has anything to do with these charges you're talking about."

"She's for real," said Rodriguez, picking up his guitar and playing softly. "You're for real. You're really something. You know, you're kind of cute. I didn't know there were any
(1) like you around any more. You're a cute kid. You get paid, don't you, whether I talk or not?"

"That isn't the point."

1. In a very real sense, Mr. Rodriguez is asking the therapist to participate in a deception: If he shows up for his therapy appointments, the police won't bother him. This places the therapist in an extraordinarily difficult position and, understandably, she is showing her impatience. However, at this point, rather than belabor the issue of his not talking, it might be more helpful to focus on the deception itself.

"What difference does it make if I sit here or some other slob?"

"The difference is, Mr. Rodriguez, that I'm here to help. I can't help you if you don't talk and won't cooperate."

"Get off it, kid."

"There's nothing to get off. You're trying to escape talking. Your body is here, Mr. Rodriguez, but that is only part of you."

"Who says my mind isn't here? It's here all right. The mind goes along with the body. Remember? They go together."

"Why have you come?"

"Didn't anyone tell you?"

"I'd like to hear it from you."

"The police."

"You mentioned the police, but I want to know why *you* want to come here." (2)

"I don't want to do anything baby. I want to live free. You get the idea – free!"

"Yes."

"Yes what?"

"Go on."

"I've been talking, baby. You're the one who isn't listening."

"I am listening."

"Listen. I'm talking." Mr. Rodriguez smiled. His hands moved quickly over the strings. "You listening? You hear now, don't you?"

"I'm afraid, Mr. Rodriguez, that there is a difference be-

2. The therapist asumes the patient has come because of emotional distress or because he wants relief from some symptoms, and she thus expects him to discuss psychological problems. The patient, however, views the situation quite differently, and the difference in their expectations blocks communication.

3 tween talking and telling me how you feel and playing the guitar."

"You're for real," said Mr. Rodriguez, leaning his head back against the wall. "You're real, kid. Real." His beaded headband slipped over his forehead and covered his eyes. "I'm talking. You get the message? I am talking loud and clear. Listen. Is it coming through, baby?"

* * *

The clinic consisted of a large store with the interior sectioned into cubicles for therapists to see patients. Plasterboard partitions gave the illusion of privacy. The central area of the store contained a row of folding chairs for patients and families, several desks, filing cabinets, and book shelves.

Patients waiting to be seen sat quietly. An infant whimpered; an older child dragged a toy car along the wall, admiring the scratches made by the metal wheels; a policeman held an adolescent by the wrist; therapists spoke to new patients; a secretary and two volunteer assistants answered telephones.

The area surrounding the clinic was heavily populated with tenements, stores, new buildings, and decaying structures scheduled for demolition. A music store next to the clinic had rigged up a street amplifying system and popular tunes blared' to a background accompaniment of automobile horns, fire engine, police, and ambulance sirens. Within the clinic, Mr. Rodriguez played his own melodies, occasionally swinging his head to toss his long hair away from his eyes.

Mr. Rodriguez had been referred to the clinic by a member of the local Narcotics Squad. He had been charged with possession of drugs but the charges were dismissed for lack of evidence. Luis Rodriguez was encouraged to get psy-

3. But of course all of us express our feelings in many ways other than talking.

chiatric help, so he had voluntarily applied to the clinic and had been assigned to Miss Lawson. 4

Twenty-three years of age, Miss Lawson, a graduate of a diploma school of nursing, had completed her baccalaureate degree and was currently enrolled in a graduate program leading to a master's degree in psychiatric nursing. As part of her clinical field experience, she worked one day a week at the store-front clinic. Mr. Rodriguez was one of three patients in her case load.

"I'm a gutter kid growing old. Who are you?" Mr. Rodriguez asked her at the next meeting.

"I'm a nurse, Mr. Rodriguez, a psychiatric nurse."

"Ever been a gutter kid?"

"Why do you ask?"

"For the simple reason that what the hell do you know 5
what it is like?"

"Know exactly what?"

"This is a bloody bore," replied Mr. Rodriguez, leaning over and playing his guitar. He refused to speak for the rest of the period.

* * *

4. The word "voluntary" obviously must be interpreted carefully. From the patient's point of view, he probably had little choice in the matter.

5. Perhaps this is also part of the patient's resistance to therapy, yet there may be a good deal of validity in his question. Surely a therapist doesn't have to live through all of a patient's experiences in order to empathically understand him. But social and cultural differences between people can indeed make communication and mutual understanding exceedingly difficult. As a first step in resolving such difficulties, it is important to understand the possible differences and appreciate their significance rather than make believe that they don't count.

Miss Lawson was admittedly surprised when he showed up for the next meeting at the exact time scheduled. She had discussed his reluctance to communicate with her supervisor. It was felt that Miss Lawson should not try to compel Mr. Rodriguez to open up, but listen to his guitar playing and perhaps try to lead into his problems through a discussion of his music.

"Perhaps you'd like to tell me something about your guitar playing?" Miss Lawson asked him at the opening of the next session.

"What do you want to know?"

"Anything you'd like to tell me."

"Is this part of your act?"

"There isn't any act."

"Come on off it," he told her. "You want me to put the guitar down and open up. I wasn't born yesterday. I've been around – a helluva lot more than you have. Remember?"

"Remember what, Mr. Rodriguez?"

He put down his guitar, slipping the strap off his shoulder. Leaning over the desk, he asked, "What do you want to know? Tell me, baby. You want my life history in forty-five minutes? It's a long story – a long continued story – kind of like a TV serial. Sometimes the strip goes frontwards with me. Now, baby, it's going backwards, up and down. See," he clapped his hands. "Interference, shadows, blocks. That's the static in the air. No antenna up. You got to turn me on
(6) before I talk. You got to find me, baby. Like the poet said," Mr. Rodriguez recited, "*Deja tu mundo, y sueña conmigo.*"

"Would you care to translate that for me?"

"It doesn't translate too well," said Mr. Rodriguez, picking up his guitar and beginning to play again.

"That's a very lovely song you're playing, Mr. Rodriguez."

6. Mr. Rodriguez is obviously bright and verbally facile, and he uses his talents to fence with the therapist.

Do you write your own music?"

"You like it?"

"Yes, very much. I believe you have real talent."

"Thanks," said Mr. Rodriguez sarcastically.

"I really meant what I said. Have you considered studying music?"

"Damn it," he shouted, "You don't need teachers. It comes from inside. Did you know that? Did you know that you don't have to go to school for everything? I suppose not. You're not the type. You're the kind who goes to school for sex. Let yourself go, Miss Lawson. Relax kid, relax. You're up tight. You're sitting there frozen. Afraid?"

He reached out and took her hand. "What are you afraid of? Don't pull back. Easy now, easy."

Miss Lawson attempted to free her hand.

"Don't you like that?"

"Let go of my hand, Mr. Rodriguez."

"After you answer, kid. Don't you like it? Perhaps just a little?"

You're going to let go of my hand."

"Go ahead. Take your hand away. I'm not stopping you."

Miss Lawson pulled her hand back.

"Rough on you?"

"What do you mean?"

"You know what I mean. You kind of liked it."

"We're here to talk about your problems, Mr. Rodriguez."

"Still on that," he laughed. "Sure. I get the idea. You're here to give me advice."

"As a nurse, yes."

"Then why in the hell don't you dress like one?"

Miss Lawson stood up and went over to open the door to the room.

"Not bad from the back – or from the front either. Come on, sit down. I get the message. I won't try anything. What do you want to know? I'll play the game. I don't want to get you in any kind of trouble. Though, between you and me, I'd try wearing something one size larger – just for kicks.

There's an old Spanish proverb. I forgot you don't speak
7 Spanish. I'll tell it to you anyway. Listen." Mr. Rodriguez played a musical background to his words. *"Tu eres mariposa aleteadora. Yo soy un hombre total."*

* * *

At the next session, Miss Lawson asked Mr. Rodriguez to sit in a chair she had placed on the other side of the desk. She sat behind the desk.

"Not taking any chances," he told her.

"How did the week go?"

"Same as usual."

"What do you do?"

"Live."

"Are you working?"

"Me?"

"Yes."

"Sure, I work."

"Would you like to tell me about what you do?"

7. Rather than pay attention to the meaning of his behavior in their sessions together, Miss Lawson continues to repeat that she and the patient are supposed to talk about his problems. Mr. Rodriguez tries to define the relationship in social-sexual terms, and finally, as if to underscore the differences between them, he ends the session with a quotation in Spanish. He talks, but in a language Miss Lawson cannot understand. Given the patient's defenses, motives for coming to the clinic, and his talent for manipulating the situation, there is perhaps little that one can reasonably hope to achieve in a brief period. Nevertheless, instead of repeating that a patient should talk about his problems, it might be more helpful in the long run to focus directly on Mr. Rodriguez's immediate behavior and attempt to achieve some understanding of it.

"I'm trying to improve my pool game. There's a shot I haven't been able to make. I thought of doing some library work."

"Mr. Rodriguez, we won't get anywhere unless you try to let me help you. What are some problems you have faced? What disturbs you?"

"I told you, kid, a pool shot. You see, there's this one shot I've been trying to make. Every time I go for it, my fingers get sweaty and I miss."

"Where do you play?"

"In a pool hall."

"Where do you sleep at night?"

"Now we're beginning to move."

"I just wanted to know if you are living with your family. Do you live alone? Are your parents in this country?"

"What parents?"

"Are they living?"

"My mother died when I was five."

"And your father?"

"He's a lottery salesman in a hill town in Puerto Rico."

"Have you seen him recently?"

"He came up last month."

"Is he still here?"

"No. He went back on a plane last week. You know those planes – little birdies in the sky, where dreams come from. I put him on the plane," said Mr. Rodriguez. "That Goddamn bundle of bones without his teeth. He has no teeth. His gums are raw and rough. You ever see rough and red raw gums? I hadn't seen him since I was twelve when he brought me up and left me here. Let him go home. Let him go home to live on his dream of a winning number. Can you imagine selling scraps of paper for a whole lifetime?" Mr. Rodriguez pulled out a lottery ticket from his pocket.

"A dream of a number. He was always going to win. He's sixty-nine and he's still going to win. Someday, he told me, his number is going to come in and he's going to have the right ticket. For the one whole week that he was here he went crazy without his numbers. He couldn't control his hands. They're used to holding numbers. A whole week without numbers and he was slobbering like a baby. Couldn't wait to get home."

"Did he come up to visit you?"

"You want the truth?'

"Yes."

"He came up because he was going to die and he was alone in the town."

"Why did you let him go back?"

"For a last chance at a winning number. He's lived for his system. I used to believe that he had a system. I asked him to tell it to me. Fat chance. He went home with his damn system."

"Our time is just about up, Mr. Rodriguez."

"You doing anything tonight?"

"I don't accept personal invitations."

"Why not?"

8 "I'm here to see you in the clinic, Mr. Rodriguez, as a patient."

"Cut the Rodriguez bit, Luis is the name."

"All right, Luis. I will see you here next week."

"How about tonight?"

"No."

"You'd like to, wouldn't you? There's a lot more to tell. Wouldn't you like to hear?"

"We can begin right where we left off next week in the clinic."

"It won't wait."

"Yes, I think it can, Luis. You can tell me next week."

8. Mr. Rodriguez's invitation is an attempt to change the nature of their relationship, and once again, rather than repeat what the patient already knows, it might have been more useful to focus on the psychological meaning of his behavior and its consequences in terms of their relationship.

Mr. Rodriguez put his guitar in its cover. He put on a suede fringed jacket.

"You didn't ask what happened to my father."

"What happened, Luis?"

"He didn't get off the plane alive. I knew he was dying. That's why I made sure he got on that plane. I didn't want him here with me. Get it? I knew he held a winning number – the one number that counts in life – and I didn't want to be around when he cashed in on the stakes. Pretty lousy of me, wasn't it? Rushed him off to that plane. Got him on and all the time I knew what was going on. Maybe tomorrow night? Are you free tomorrow night?" he asked.

* * *

Mr. Rodriguez did not come for his next appointment. Miss Lawson waited for him, and after the time had passed, she asked the secretary to telephone his home. A call was made, and the secretary was told that no one by the name of Luis Rodriguez had ever lived there. The receiver was slammed down.

Miss Lawson tried herself later that morning, and a young male voice admitted knowing Luis but insisted that he hadn't seen him in some time and refused to give any further information. Miss Lawson wrote a letter to Luis, and the letter was returned to the clinic with a scrawled note to the effect that the party was unknown. Miss Lawson decided to wait another week to see if Luis would keep his scheduled appointment. He did not appear.

Concerned about him, Miss Lawson talked about the case with her supervisor, Mrs. Danelle, and the clinic director, Mrs. Engle. She explained that Luis had been so regular that his unexplained absence concerned her. She wondered if something had happened and felt a responsibility to check on his whereabouts.

"You can't go chasing patients in their homes," said Mrs. Engle.

"It's not a matter of chasing. Luis simply isn't like that.
9 He was a most intelligent, serious young man. He really wanted to be helped. I felt that. I felt him reaching out and that's exactly why I am bothered. He would come if something hadn't happened to prevent him. We took on the case and we should see it through."

"Now wait a minute. We take on cases here in the clinic. But we're only indirectly responsible for the people when they are on the streets. We help; we try to help them but we can't go ordering other peoples' lives around," said Mrs. Engle.

"I don't want to order his life. That's absurd. You mean if a patient stops coming without any warning, we just let the case drop? That isn't right."

"What isn't right?"

"That we stop our responsibility at the front door. People live outside of those doors, Mrs. Engle. They have lives elsewhere. Yes, we're one small part of their lives, but sometimes the smaller bits can make the difference."

"How was Luis with you?" asked Mrs. Danelle.

"Responsive."

"Did he tell you anything about himself?"

"He was beginning to. I will say the first few weeks I couldn't get him to say anything. He did resist. I waited it out. And then the last meeting he opened up, or started to."

"What did he tell you?"

"About his father, his life. He might have some guilt feelings about his father, I don't know. He said he hadn't seen his father since he was twelve. His mother died when he

9. In the light of her previous experience with Mr. Rodriguez, the statement "He really wanted to be helped" appears to reflect some distortion. Mr. Rodriguez may indeed want help, but Miss Lawson's statement leads one to consider the possible counter-transference feelings of the therapist for the patient.

was five. He's lived his whole life here alone."

"Did he say that?"

"No, but I gather he didn't have much of a home life. He's wandering. He said he's trying to find himself. He's twenty-nine and he seems much younger, I think. He's so lost."

"Did he tell you he felt lost?"

"Yes and no. One thing I know is that he didn't want to leave our interviews. He asked me to see him outside of the clinic."

"What did you say?" asked Mrs. Danelle.

"I told him that was impossible."

"How did he take it?"

"He didn't do anything, but that is why I am upset. He had been so silent; then he opened up and told me a few things, and I said I couldn't see him outside the clinic. What worries me is that he didn't understand my explanation and he might interpret my not wanting to see him as a rejection of him personally." (10)

She continued saying that she really thought it right to contact him and to explain that she wanted to see him in the clinic and could even arrange to see him more than once a week if that was necessary, but that she could not see him outside of the clinic.

"I feel so up in the air about him," she told the supervisor and the director. "It just ended. It doesn't seem right. I mean, we were beginning to talk. He's not just any kind of

10. At this point, problems of counter-transference are apparent as Miss Lawson's concern seems to be over-determined and her reactions influenced to a large extent by her own feelings. This does not mean that therapists should not be realistically concerned about their patients or that their concern stops at the office door. But one must carefully distinguish between reality-based concern and reactions that stem largely from the therapist's own feelings and conflicts.

beatnik from the street. He's quite a sensitive young man. He plays the guitar magnificently. I was impressed. I've tried taking guitar lessons, so I have some idea about how good he is. And he has a fantastic literary knowledge. He loves to quote poetry. He really needs some help, and I do feel worried."

Mrs. Engle said that Miss Lawson might have communicated more than professional involvement with Luis. "Remember how he might see it," explained Mrs. Danelle. "You're an attractive young woman; he's an appealing young man. I wonder if this is what's bothering you."

"That wasn't the case at all," insisted Miss Lawson. "I won't say he wasn't attractive, but the relationship *was* definitely a professional one on my part – certainly that and nothing more."

Miss Lawson said she might make one more effort to reach him by letter. "If he returns to the clinic," Mrs. Danelle said, "he must be assigned to another therapist."

That afternoon Miss Lawson wrote a brief, formal note to Luis, inquiring about his welfare and suggesting that he continue coming to the clinic. She personally delivered the letter to his home address, which was several blocks away from the clinic. An elderly woman answered the doorbell and took the letter. Although she spoke little English, she was able to tell Miss Lawson that Luis was sick and in Depester Hospital. She asked Miss Lawson why she wanted to see Luis.

"He's no good. You'll be hurt," she warned Miss Lawson.

"I'm not here on a personal call." Miss Lawson tried to explain her position, but the woman shook her head and slammed the door.

Three weeks after Luis Rodriguez's last clinic visit, he telephoned Miss Lawson and asked her if she would come and visit him in Depester Hospital. The large hospital complex included both the medical and psychiatric facilities that served the various community mental health clinics, half-way houses, and other social agencies.

That afternoon Miss Lawson went to the hospital and spoke to Mr. Gordon, an attendant who worked on the tenth floor ward where Mr. Rodriguez had been placed. She explained that she had been seeing Mr. Rodriguez at a store-front clinic and had recently learned that he had been hospitalized.

"There, too," commented Mr. Gordon.

"What do you mean?"

"You know much about Luis?"

"Some. He told me a few things about his background."

"Don't tell me," said Mr. Gordon. "I can hear him. Down and out Luis. Poor misunderstood Luis. If only his mother had loved him, life would have been different. What else did he tell you?"

"That he was from Puerto Rico and about his father. He's had a difficult life, Mr. Gordon. It's not been an easy way for Luis. He's a very sensitive young man."

"Don't tell me how sensitive he is. We all know Luis. He's one of our regular old patients. You can count on Luis. He's been in and out of here, oh, I'd say, going on ten years. Ten years, young lady. And when he isn't around here we know Luis is over telling his sob story at some other clinic. What line did he hand you? The one about being an actor?"

"No."

"I know, don't tell me. He gave you the musician line."

"He does play the guitar."

"Luis doesn't play the guitar. He's an unrecognized star if you listen to him. If he only had money; if he only had time; if he only had a teacher, he would be great. There's one thing Luis forgets, and that is you need talent."

"He has talent, Mr. Gordon. I've heard him play. He's got a great deal of potential talent."

"You know anything really about guitar playing? I bet not. Luis is third rate. I think things are beginning to catch up on him. When did you last see him?"

"Three weeks ago."

"Was he shooting up then?"

"Luis wasn't on narcotics, Mr. Gordon."

"Now Luis wouldn't do that sort of thing. Maybe he was clean when you saw him. That's not the way he came in here. He's on his way. We'll keep him awhile and then let him out. Luis will be back pushing. I told him, though, we weren't going to take his pals coming in here passing the stuff. We had our hands full last time he was here. His gang was in here selling to everybody the minute our back was turned."

"If you can't do anything here for him, why aren't you referring him somewhere so he can get help? Luis wants and needs help."

"Reform him? You didn't know Luis too long, did you?"

"I said refer him and maybe reform him. He only came to the clinic for a few months. He was just beginning to open up and then he stopped coming."

"I know his line. He needed you. You were the one who really understood him. You had true feelings. You could see what he was trying to express. Come on, what else did he hand you?"

"Nothing else. Mr. Gordon, I believed him. He's had a difficult life."

"You believed him? You couldn't see through him? You mean you really believed his line? A hard life. You know
(11) what his hard life has been – mugging for purses on Sylvester Street – little old ladies. A hard life. Two kids, one's four and

11. Mr. Gordon's reaction is in dramatic contrast to Miss Lawson's, and one is tempted to evaluate his view as more realistic than hers. Yet in his own way, Mr. Gordon's countertransference problems are as evident as those of Miss Lawson. One emphasizes strengths and the other emphasizes weaknesses. Both, of course, are right: Luis is indeed bright and sensitive, and he probably is also psychopathic. But both, too, are wrong insofar as the narrowness of their views has distorted the total picture. In any case, neither unrealistic optimism nor total pessimism is likely to be very helpful to the patient.

the other's three — a hard life. I got the two mothers coming here every week ready to kill him. A hard life. Listen, what did you say your name was — Miss Lawson, that guy has never worked a day in his life. He's lived off the streets, off people like you. I don't mean we shouldn't help him. I don't mean that at all. But this soft sister bit — weeping for Luis, who would steal your last dime — I don't think that's the way. He's been no angel here. You want to see him? He's playing pool. He's pretty mad now because we won't let him have his guitar.

"Why not? The guitar meant so much to him."

"Because if something happens to the guitar the city gets sued for personal property being damaged. You should see the lawsuits we got from patients."

Luis was playing pool at a table in front of the elevators. Two attendants were seated opposite the elevator doors watching to see that patients did not leave the floor.

Luis continued to shoot pool. He walked around the table and said to Miss Lawson, "Got a cigarette?"

"No."

"Nice to see you."

"How have you been, Luis?"

"Fine. What else?"

"I wondered why you didn't show up for your appointments."

"Now you know."

"You will get good care here, Luis."

"Sure. Miss me?"

"We wondered what happened."

"This is it, kid. This is it baby — the real thing."

"That's a good shot, Luis."

"Good shot, but the wrong one for this game. Say, you got any pull around here?

"You don't need any pull. You just have to be straight, Luis. What is it you want?"

Luis walked over to her. "My guitar. You got to tell them. I need my guitar. See my fingers." He fluttered his fingers.

"They're crying, baby, crying. You ever see crying fingers? I got to have it. You be a good baby. Get it for me. I don't forget favors. I'm coming out in a few weeks. Will you be doing anything? Just where we left off. How about it?" said Luis, hunching his shoulders. He grinned at Miss Lawson while he plucked an imaginary guitar, his shoulders swaying, his left foot in a hospital slipper tapping a steady rhythm.

"WHERE DID YOU GROW UP?"

1. Luis Rodriguez refuses to speak to Miss Lawson for the first sessions and only plays his guitar. Miss Lawson feels he is hiding behind his guitar. Do you agree? Do you feel that the guitar is a form of communication for Luis? Have you had any experiences with patients who have utilized forms of communication systems other than verbal? What types of nonverbal communication systems did they employ?

2. Miss Lawson persists in trying to get Luis to talk. How do you feel about her direct approach to Luis? Would you have reacted similiarly?

3. Luis is twenty-nine and Miss Lawson is twenty-three. Considering Luis' background, how do you think he perceives Miss Lawson? How does he try to relate to her? What can Miss Lawson do to deal with the situation? What would you do if you were in a similar situation? Given the circumstances of this case do you believe that Miss Lawson can realistically hope to relate to Luis on a therapeutic basis?

4. Luis insists that he is talking through his music. How do you interpret this statement? What is your opinion about Luis' insistence that he is talking and Miss Lawson is not listening?

5. Luis and Miss Lawson have grown up in completely different social and cultural environments. Do you feel that it is necessary for patients and therapists to have the same

social and cultural orientation? Why might the differences create barriers? Conversely, how might these differences enhance rapport?

6. Miss Lawson is told to try to reach Luis through his music. Miss Lawson makes an attempt. How does Luis interpret her interest? What is his reaction?

7. The controversy of whether patients feel more comfortable relating to professionals who are not in uniform has not been resolved. Do you think Luis might have responded differently to Miss Lawson if she had worn a uniform? Do you believe the uniform enhances or deters the establishment of trust and confidence on the part of a patient?

8. Luis reveals some facts about his background and at the same time tries to persuade Miss Lawson to see him socially. Have you been in a situation in which the patient tried to establish a social relationship with you? How have you handled the situation?

9. Mrs. Engle, the clinic director, and Mrs. Danelle, the supervisor, feel that Miss Lawson has developed a personal interest in Luis that goes beyond her professional role. Do you feel they have misinterpreted Miss Lawson's comments about Luis? What is your evaluation of Miss Lawson's attitude toward Luis? Concerned about his failure to keep appointments, Miss Lawson makes several attempts to contact him. Do you think she acted correctly? Do you feel that she should have permitted Luis to terminate the visits without attempting to persuade him to return?

10. In contrast to Miss Lawson's perception of Luis as a troubled but talented young man, Mr. Gordon presents a totally different picture. How do you interpret these radical differences in perception? How do you perceive Luis?

7

The Christmas Party

Early in December, Dr. Tanner, a staff psychiatrist, talked to the nursing staff, attendants, and other paraprofessional employees about the relationship between mental health and holidays. "It is important," he stated, "for all of us to understand that for some individuals holidays may be psychologically threatening. Statistics indicate that incidences of depression, suicide, psychosomatic complaints, and various acting-out behaviors increase significantly during these times. Although we might like to believe that people look forward to holidays as a source of pleasure, we must remember that for those individuals who feel alienated from families, friends, or society, holidays may be viewed from a totally different perspective. Rather than occasions for celebration, these special days may induce stress and personal crises."

Miss Cifano's reaction to the lecture was immediate. During a morning coffee break she talked about her feelings with several staff nurses.

"What Dr. Tanner said really hit me."

"Why should you be so upset?" asked Miss Rivlen.

"I'm not upset, but what he said suddenly made sense to me," explained Miss Cifano. "Haven't you ever noticed how patients behave around holidays?"

"In my opinion," answered Miss Rivlen, "he always exaggerates. He always tells some dramatic story. You have to take what he says with a grain of salt. Between you and me, patients on Five couldn't care less if it was the Fourth of July or the fourth of December. We have some who don't even know the dates of their own birthdays, let alone worrying about whether it's a national holiday."

"I don't think he meant *any* holiday," insisted Miss Cifano." I think the point he was making was about a big holiday like Christmas. None of you worked here last year on Christmas Eve," she said to the nurses seated around the table. "I did. I was here. You know what happened? Nothing. The patients sat around and watched television."

"They like television," commented Miss Derman.

"But it was Christmas Eve. I had to work. You were all home with families. Don't tell me the patients *wanted* to watch television shows about happy Christmases when they were just sitting here without anything really unusual."

"Maybe you felt that way. Maybe the patients couldn't have cared less," suggested Miss Rivlen.

"I don't agree. I brought in a little Christmas tree. Patients kept coming over and telling me how pretty the little tree was. I even remember that one lady started crying and asked me about presents. I had to tell her there weren't any presents – just a tree for decoration."

'That doesn't mean she was going psychotic because of Christmas," said Miss Derman. "She made an association. That's all. She saw a tree and she wanted a present. That seems perfectly reasonable to me."

"How can you say that?" retorted Miss Cifaro. "How can you possibly think our patients aren't concerned about Christmas? Just because they don't say anything or aren't doing anything doesn't mean that the holiday isn't on their minds. How about you?" she asked Miss Derman. "Aren't you beginning to think of Christmas?"

"I'm beginning to worry about money, if that's what you mean. If anyone else gets a husband, wife, or baby between now and December twenty-fourth, you can bet your life they're not going to be added to my list. They wait until next year."

"But that's the point! These people haven't any lists. Some of these patients aren't on anybody's lists; chances are they're never going to be."

"Look, honey," said Miss Rivlen, "Don't you get any ideas about getting them presents. Not on my salary, that's for sure."

"I'm not asking you to do anything like that. But we *could* do something. We could make Christmas meaningful in lots of other ways. I just don't feel the staff does *all* they can. We need *everyone* very much involved."

"Isn't there a special Christmas dinner?" asked another of the staff.

"More cranberry sauce," responded Miss Cifaro angrily.

"Come on now," said Miss Rivlen. "Hold off the sentiment. Who wants more coffee?" She volunteered to take empty cups for refills.

Miss Cifano crumbled crusts of bread on her plate. She had worked on the psychiatric unit for just over a year. Last Christmas was her first experience on the ward during a major holiday. Her only previous contact with psychiatric patients had been during training. Because she was the staff member with the least seniority, she had been asked to work Christmas Eve. Dr. Tanner's remarks evoked memories of a dismal experience which had lingered in her mind for weeks. Of all the holidays, she felt that Christmas alone captured everyone's imagination and spirit. The period in her own life was characterized by enjoyable activities: detailed preparations, shopping excursions and total family involvement.

After Miss Rivlen distributed second cups of coffee, Miss Cifano said emphatically, "You can call it sentiment. You know, I don't care what you call it. But what is so wrong with trying to do something special? We could try. You can laugh at me," she told Miss Rivlen, "but you know, I wonder if you did do something here, maybe your own Christmas would be just that more rewarding."

"I don't think I enjoy sermons at a Monday morning coffee hour," Miss Rivlen told Miss Cifano. "Meanwhile, I'll let you people plan for snowmen and elves; I have patients to take care of – medications to pass out. When I took this job no one told me playing Santa Claus was part of my duties."

The others remained with Miss Cifano. In general, they felt that her idea might be a good one, but they wanted to know more about what she had in mind before they would make any decisions about participating. Miss Derman felt that Miss Cifano had been biting to Miss Rivlen. "You know she's the one around here who is the first to cover for someone. It hardly seemed fair of you to have told her off."

Miss Cifano agreed that she had spoken abruptly and said she would apologize later. "I guess her attitude threw me," she admitted. "You just mention an idea, and she's the first to take it and twist it into something funny."

"Oh, that's her way," Miss Derman told her. "She doesn't mean it."

That afternoon Miss Cifano discussed her project with Mrs. Burney, the nursing supervisor.

"I'd like to do something very special here at the hospital about Christmas."

"Yourself?" asked Mrs. Burney.

"Not myself. I expect to do most of the work because it is my idea, but I think some of the staff would volunteer help. I would like to have patients make decorations. I also thought the psychodrama group could plan a program. We could get patient choral groups started." Miss Cifano excitedly outlined a number of possible suggestions.

"The plan sounds like a good one to me," Mrs. Burney said. "We have never had anything quite like what you describe. I recall years ago we had a volunteer group come over and pass out candy and cookies and sing carols. I seem to remember the patients enjoyed themselves. I don't know what the attitude would be nowadays. We've a different type of patient."

"They may be different in some respects, but I know they aren't any different when it comes to feelings about Christmas."

"You may be right. But there are problems."

"How do you mean?" asked Miss Cifano.

"You mentioned something about having staff involved. We're already facing a staffing problem."

"I thought these Christman plans could be part of our regular routine. I wanted to have all my plans part of regular activities."

"On paper," answered Mrs. Burney, "your idea sounds fine. But there are only so many hours, and we still have ongoing routines. You can't expect people to drop whatever they're presently doing."

"They wouldn't have to drop anything," argued Miss Cifano. "We could just have all plans revolve around a
(1) Christmas theme. I have a psychodrama group. We could get started right away on Christmas skits. We could have some extra meetings as time went on."

"Extra. That's what I mean. You said that your plans would be integrated into the program, and now you talk in terms of extras."

"Well then, during free time. Patients spend hours sitting around anyway. We could put that free time to good use."

1. One certainly can't fault Miss Cifano for her positive hopes and aspirations, but as her enthusiasm builds, she seems to be losing sight of the impact her behavior might have on others. Just as anyone very excited by an idea tends to see everything in relation to that idea, Miss Cifano's world is beginning to revolve around her plans for the Christmas party. Others, of course, do not share her enthusiasm, and conflicts may very well arise from differences in points of view.

"The staff members would have to decide if that's what they want to do," said Mrs. Burney.

"I never dreamed anyone would be *made* to help. I think they would all want to help," replied Miss Cifano.

"Oh, I'm sure some will and some won't," answered Mrs. Burney. "Have you thought about expense?"

"There wouldn't be any expense."

"But you'd want decorations, and I suppose some candy and cake."

"I also thought of presents. Small presents for the patients."

"Where would these come from?" asked Mrs. Burney. "We're already running into a deficit as it is. I've spent hours with the administration trying to cut next year's costs. I don't think anyone at the comptroller's office would jump with Christmas spirit if I told them I needed money for patient presents!"

"That isn't any problem at all," said Miss Cifano. She told Mrs. Burney that she had discussed her ideas with her parish priest, and he would be happy to announce her project to various church organizations. He felt that the parishioners would respond gladly to appeals for donations.

"I have a feeling," said Miss Cifano, "our problem won't be getting materials, presents, decorations; we're going to end up having too much!"

"I don't want to spoil your excitement," said Mrs. Burney, "but I think you ought to wait and see. I have found that people get all worked up and enthusiastic, but when the time comes to really give, they forget. It's funny how easily people can forget. But then I don't know your parish. I gather a lot of this activity is going to revolve around getting ready for a Christmas Eve party and a Christmas Day celebration."

"That's right," said Miss Cifano.

"Have you thought about who will be here?"

"The patients."

"Oh, I know the patients who don't have passes to go home will be here. But you're going to need staff. Everyone

has requested those days off. I planned only to have a skeleton staff working those shifts. I've been up nights trying to think of how to arrange for time off. Everyone has a perfectly good reason why they deserve those days. Someone has a sick grandmother. Another person lives five hundred
2 miles away and wants to get home. There are staff with families, children; I can't expect those people to give up Christmas with their own families to work at the hospital."

"I'll work," replied Miss Cifano.

"But you worked last year and only two weeks ago you were in here reminding me that you worked last year and wanted to be sure that you were off this Christmas."

"But not any more," answered Miss Cifano. "This is my idea, and I can assure you that I expect to be here seeing that the project is a success."

"Well, in that case," said Mrs. Burney, "I can't see any reason to tell you not to go ahead. I suggest you try. See how the plans move along. You can always change your mind, I suppose."

"I won't change my mind," replied Miss Cifano. "Mrs. Burney, if I undertake this plan, I intend to carry it through. I was here last year. It was awful. I am going to make sure that it is different this year. Everyone will want to help. I can't but believe that the patients won't become involved.

2. Mrs. Burney's perspective obviously differs a good deal from that of Miss Cifano's. Mrs. Burney sees all the practical problems that the Christmas party might entail, and it seems as if the more enthusiasic Miss Cifano becomes, the more problems Mrs. Burney brings up. It would probably be unfair to interpret Mrs. Burney's response as obstructive; after all, the problems she raises are real. However, it is also true that Miss Cifano's enthusiasm itself might have elicited Mrs. Burney's problem-oriented response, in that she may have interpreted the enthusiasm as an indication of Miss Cifano's unrealistic expectations.

And I know the staff feel strongly about Christmas. If everyone does just something, it will be great."

Miss Cifano contacted all members of the staff and explained her plans for a Christmas celebration, asking for their cooperation.

"I don't know what I can do," said Miss Derman. "I can't sing; I can't sew a button on without sticking my own thumb. Seriously," she told Miss Cifano, "the plan sounds like fun, but I never was in a play in my life, much less help make one up."

"I don't want you to make up a play or perform. I thought you could have your group make up their own play. You know, read a story or act it out."

"Do you know which group I have?" asked Miss Derman. "I guess you don't. I have eight people. Four stopped speaking ten years ago. There are five schizophrenics and three depressed patients. Now tell me what idea for a play could I present to them? I don't think some of them know I'm in the room, and I've had this group for six months. It's getting so I'm behaving like them. I just go sit in a chair against the wall."

Although Miss Derman made light of her group and the reactions of the people, she told another nurse later that it was really unfair of Miss Cifano to have put her on the spot.

"I kept trying to tell her I had a rough group. I think she got the idea I didn't want to help. It makes me out some
sort of Scrooge. Sure I think having something for the pa- (3)
tients is important. But she has a different group. She has people who talk. You can't shut some of them up. I ended

3. Miss Derman's reaction underscores the importance of perspective in interpreting and reacting to a given situation. From Miss Cifano's point of view, giving a Christmas play means fun and involvement in a meaningful activity; from Miss Derman's perspective, giving a Christmas play is an impossible burden.

up with the nontalkers and now she tells me I'm to get them to make up a Christmas play. I haven't been able to get some of them to look at each other, let alone write a script."

The dance therapist thought Miss Cifano's idea was excellent. In fact, she said that she had been thinking about something along the same lines. She was introducing light Christmas music and having the patients move interpretively to the music. Some very interesting results had begun to emerge. For example, she had patients pretending to be unfolding branches of a tree. One woman had pretended to be a mechanical doll and another patient wound her up; all movements were coordinated with a children's record about presents to be received at Christmas.

Miss Young, a staff nurse, and Miss Johnson, an attendant who managed the patient beauty shop, discovered a mutual interest in singing. Both were members of their respective church choirs. In response to Miss Cifano's request, they volunteered to form a patient mixed chorus. A time was set and practice sessions for interested patients began in earnest. After a week of rehearsals, several nonsinging patients complained to Mrs. Burney that they hadn't had their hair washed. Others reported they had been rushed and soap was left in their hair.

When Mrs. Burney questioned her, Miss Johnson said, "I've been doing the heads, but we've had caroling practice in the morning so there is sometimes a jam up in the afternoons, but I get around to everyone."

Two other nurses on duty with Miss Young felt they were doing her work. "We know she's working hard on the Christmas carols but we were terribly shorthanded this morning. We had four new patients to get settled and Young was in the dayroom singing 'Jingle Bells'."

* * *

Because of staff concerns about the nature of participation and the implications such activities had with regard to routine duties and time off, Mrs. Burney posted the following announcement on the staff bulletin board:

Any staff member who chooses to help with Christmas plans for the patients should note that this work is voluntary *and must* not *interfere with regular assignments or routines. No one is expected to work overtime. Schedule of assignments for holiday days off has nothing to do with any plans for hospital parties.*

If there are any other questions, please see me. Although Miss Cifano's Christmas plan has my approval and good wishes, I do want you to know that this is an independent activity. The hospital is NOT sponsoring the program nor is anyone requesting or expecting staff involvement. You are free to do as you wish. Let's look forward to a very happy and joyous holiday season. Mrs. Burney, Nursing Supervisor.

"I think that notice is terribly unfair," Miss Cifano told Mrs. Burney.

"Unfair?" Mrs. Burney was obviously surprised. 4

"It's just the way you said it. Everyone has been so helpful and the notice sounds like you don't agree with the idea or at least don't feel that it is important. It is so *terribly* important."

4. Mrs. Burney is indeed faced with a real problem; routine duties must be continued while special activities for the Christmas party go on. Miss Cifano is probably reacting primarily to the form of Mrs. Burney's response: the public notice and implied reprimand rather than a personal chat about the problems that have arisen. Thus, the relationships among staff members have become increasingly strained. Beginning with very positive intentions and a potentially fine idea, Miss Cifano's inability to see other points of view has resulted in problems for others. These, in turn, have evoked a sense of frustration, resentment, and

"You are misinterpreting the notice," said Mrs. Burney. "I suggest you don't get carried away. Remember this is a hospital for patients and not a playground. Our job is to help these people regain mental health, not to amuse them."

* * *

An important aspect of Miss Cifano's planning consisted of preparations for decorations. Corridors and rooms of the hospital were a stark white. Gray steel doors barricaded exits. Windows of many of the rooms were either bare or covered with worn plastic curtains. Miss Cifano wanted the areas transformed, and she outlined extensive decorating plans to Mr. Halberstrom and Miss Liane, the two occupational therapists.

"It all sounds grand," said Miss Liane, smiling.

"I don't see what is humorous," said Miss Cifano.

"Well, you keep talking about trees and wreaths and cut-out candy canes, and I just did an inventory of our supplies. We have six pieces of material for carry-all bags, seven balls of mismatched yarn and some other scraps. I've been sitting here and listening to what you want us to make and it just sounds funny when I think of what we have in the way of materials."

"I am planning on getting materials."

"You are?" asked Mr. Halberstrom. "How? After eight months of delays, I finally got my order for new woodworking tools." He showed Miss Liane and Miss Cifano hammers, saws, and other assorted woodcarving tools, "This

anger in others, and Miss Cifano interprets their reactions as unreasonable in the light of her own positive intentions. At this point it would probably have been helpful to discuss the growing difficulties with all those involved, clarifying their communications with each other before further misperceptions and misinterpretations developed.

is the first decent equipment I've had since I started working here fifteen years ago."

Mr. Halberstrom and Miss Liane agreed that any patient who was interested and who was not currently involved on a project would be encouraged to work on Chrismas decorations. Miss Cifano told them they would be supplied with all necessary materials.

"When you bring in the supplies," said Miss Liane, "we can see what can be done."

Miss Cifano contacted her parish priest, who relayed her request for Christmas contributions to various church-sponsored organizations. During the following week, Miss Cifano went to the church directly after dinner every night to supervise the collection of donations. Within a few days she had cartons filled with clothing, gifts, baked goods, and a wide variety of Christmas ornaments, nativity displays, and other holiday decorations. On a Sunday evening, Miss Cifano enlisted the help of several friends, and the boxes were delivered to the hospital. The night attendant opened the door of the occupational therapy room, and the boxes were stored on shelves, tables, chairs, and along one end of the room.

On Monday morning when Miss Cifano arrived for work Mrs. Burney greeted her angrily.

"What went on here last night? You were here. I was told you were here by the patints. What went on?"

"With patients?"

"Not with patients. I'm beginning to think we have more trouble with staff than we do with patients. I can't understand why you didn't get permission."

"For what?"

"For what? The boxes! Mr. Halberstrom and Miss Liane are up in arms. You'll have to straighten this out with them. I went down myself and I can't blame them. They're fit to be tied. You better go explain to them."

"But I didn't do anything. All we did was put the boxes in the O.T. room. They're for the Christmas party. Lots of the materials in there are what they will need to work on for the decorations."

"You mean you didn't check with Mr. Halberstrom? That's
(5) what he said. I wanted to verify this with you first. I couldn't believe that you would just go ahead and put the boxes in his room without asking permission."

Miss Cifano went down to the occupational therapy room where the patients were gathering for a morning class. Several had opened boxes of clothing, and two women clug tenaciously to a sweater, arguing that each was the first to touch the sweater and therefore was the owner.

"You musn't open the boxes." Miss Cifano tried to take the sweater from the women. "This is a surprise for Christmas. You'll have to wait. You wouldn't want to spoil Christmas. You mustn't open the boxes. Who told you to open the boxes?" she asked one of the women.

"Mr. Halberstrom said we could. He said he wanted them out of here." The patient refused to relinquish the sweater.

"If you take the sweater now," said Miss Cifano, "then at Christmas you will just have to go without getting a gift."

Mr. Halberstrom told the woman to go ahead and keep the sweater.

"See what you've caused?" he said to Miss Cifano. "For an hour now I've had these people fighting over the boxes. You're just lucky you came in now or I would have let them hand everything out."

"They're for Christmas."

"I know they're for Christmas, but what about my classes until then? You just can't come in and take over like this.

5. As in any social organization, people in this hospital have certain "territories" which are, in a sense, their domain. For one person, it may be a desk; for another, a bed; for Mr. Halberstrom, the O.T. room. Thus, from a psychological point of view, Miss Cifano has invaded his territory and, regardless of her good intentions, he is understandably angry.

Do you realize that I have two hammers and a saw missing? I have six men wanting to finish bookends. Do you know that if those hammers and the saw are lost, I can't requisition others? They were new this fall. All my woodworking tools were new. They had been on order for six months. We finally got them budgeted for and now they disappear. "Here," he said to a patient, "you just have to keep on sandpapering. How do you think he feels? Mr. Appel has been working for four weeks on those bookends. I told him he could hammer them together this morning, and now I discover I haven't any hammers or nails."

"I didn't touch the tools," insisted Miss Cifano.

"Then where are they? They were here when I locked up on Friday."

"We didn't take any tools."

"Who opened the door? Where did you get a key?"

"Mr. Davis opened the door."

"I'm going to have to tell him. *No one* is to come into this room without my permission. Now get everything out of here." (6)

"But these boxes have the materials for the Christmas decorations."

Mr. Halberstrom and Miss Liane began lifting the cartons off the shelves. The box of woodworking tools was found.

"You did agree to help," said Miss Cifano.

"In the mood I'm in I don't think I want to talk about it," answered Mr. Halberstrom. "You'll have to clear this stuff out so we can use our tables and shelves."

With the help of the patients, the boxes were carried down to the nurse's station and into the nursing office.

"They can't stay here," said Mrs. Burney.

"Temporarily – I'll find a place."

6. As the interaction between Miss Cifano and Mr. Halberstrom progresses, it becomes increasingly evident that he is reacting primarily to the invasion of his private territory.

"All right, but I haven't any idea where you're going to find storage space."

Space was located in the hospital basement, and the boxes were taken down. "Do you realize," said Mrs. Burney, "you have spent all morning on those boxes?"

During lunch hour, Miss Cifano talked to Miss Liane and showed her the materials for red and green curtains, Christmas ornaments, and other decorations. Miss Liane agreed to start some of the women working, although, as she told Miss Cifano, many lacked patience or skill.

"Let them do what they can," said Miss Cifano. "Whatever they do will be important to them." She suggested that patients who weren't able to paint, paste, or glue should be encouraged to draw pictures that could be hung in the corridors and day rooms.

Miss Liane agreed that she would talk to Mr. Halberstrom when he quieted down. Perhaps he could be convinced to help out and get some of the male patients working on simple projects.

However, she wasn't too hopeful. "He's not in much of a mood to work on holiday decorations." She also told Miss Cifano that Mr. Halberstrom had said "yes" because Miss Cifano had been so excited and he hadn't wanted to put a damper on her excitement. "But he has a point," explained Miss Liane. "I also said 'yes,' but afterwards I realized that the patients do have things they have been working on. I think it's important for their sense of self-accomplishment to finish a task they've already begun." Nevertheless, Miss Liane consented to make an effort.

The idea of helping to decorate the floor for Christmas was introduced to the patients at the scheduled occupational classes. Many patients responded eagerly and were assigned tasks of sewing red and green panels of material into curtains, repainting ornaments, or twisting sprigs of evergreen into simple wreaths. Some patients lingered after the class to work on the projects.

After an initial burst of enthusiasm, interest waned.

Several patients who had partially completed wreaths or cut out candy canes suddenly decided to return to their original projects. Those who continued to labor over Christmas decorations resented those who preferred working on their own handicrafts.

"Selfish, that's what they are," complained one patient, Mrs. Tiller. "I don't see why we got to slave for them. It don't make sense. Some people does all the work and others just sit back and take what they don't earn. You get people who don't help, then they got no right to join in the fun." She told Miss Cifano that she was "boiling over." "You got to make everyone do something," she told Miss Cifano.

"But that isn't the Christmas spirit," Miss Cifano replied.

"Don't you give me none of that spirit talk. I got that from my family all my life. Why in the hell do you think I'm here? Because it was *me* who *did* all the time, while they took and they kept taking until I couldn't stand it no more. That's how it is. Some people do all and then they fall flat; others just stay where they is – going and going. You don't work, then you don't come to the party." She threw down a Santa Claus cardboard figure. "I think I'll just be like the rest. Sit back, Mrs. Tiller, I say to myself, sit back. You come to the party like a lady."

"It's not who does what that counts," Miss Cifano told her. "That isn't the idea. We all have to cooperate. Christmas is for everyone. You can't take that attitude. We all have to help in whatever way we can. Just because someone on the staff doesn't do as much as I am doing doesn't mean they can't share the pleasure in having the halls and rooms decorated. Christmas is for all of us. If you can do more than someone else, you should just feel good about it, not resentful."

° ° °

Two weeks before Christmas Miss Rivlen told Miss Cifano that the whole idea she had introduced was having a detrimental effect on a few patients.

"You know," she told Miss Cifano, "not everyone around here celebrates Christmas."

"How do you mean?"

"I mean some people don't believe in Christmas. They have other religious beliefs."

"But that doesn't mean they can't enjoy Christmas."

"Maybe you better tell my patients that. They don't see your point."

"Who?'

"I'll tell you who," answered Miss Rivlen. "Mrs. Salomon for one. She has been doing beautifully. I can't tell you how happy I have been with her progress. You didn't know her as well as I did. This woman came here six months ago in horrible shape. She's in my group. We had finally started to communicate. Maybe you should know that she's back right where we started – crying constantly. You can't look at her before she starts weeping."

"And you're trying to blame this on Christmas? You never wanted to help out. I knew this from the first day. You went around telling the others it was a silly idea. Of course, anything that means any extra time, any effort would be silly. Well, I don't happen to view my work in terms of time
(7) and money. I think when I reach that point, it's about time to quit and do something else in life."

"Why don't you go and talk to Mrs. Salomon? Then when you finish with her I'll send you around to a few other pa-

7. The argument has obviously gone far beyond the Christmas party and the care of patients. As a consequence of anger evoked, the specific issue has become generalized to a matter of professional competence. This is the point at which angry conflicts become especially difficult to resolve; one might be able to deal reasonably with the particulars of a specific problem, but issues like professional competence are likely to lead to even greater anger and conflict.

tients." said Miss Rivlen. "I've been here a few years longer than you have – just a few, like maybe ten. Don't you go around and criticize me in terms of my effort."

That afternoon Miss Cifano visited Mrs. Salomon in her room. She was sitting on her bed weeping and refused to talk to Miss Cifano. Another patient in the room said, "She been like that for a couple of days now. Miss Rivlen gave her something. But it don't do her no good."

"Why are you crying, Mrs. Salomon? Would you like to talk to me about it?"

"She don't want to talk to no one," said the other patient. She beckoned the nurse over to a corner of the room. "She won't do no talking. But I think I know why," whispered the patient.

"I'd like you to tell me," replied Miss Cifano.

"Maybe you would and maybe you wouldn't. You're taken with these Christmas plans. I never was much for the day, but then maybe when you know that it was nothing but mittens and scarves, and you wanted something big, like I wanted a doll and my brother wanted a bike and there was the mittens and scarves, you don't want to think much about the day. But Mrs. Salomon got other reasons. She got a different religion. She told me she won't come to no holiday party for Christmas. She says we're doing this to make her miserable. I told her this holiday never made me happy and I'm Christian."

Miss Cifano went back to Mrs. Salomon's bedside. The other patient left the room. "You don't have to cry," said Miss Cifano. "I'm sorry you misunderstood about the holiday. But Christmas is for everyone to share. It's the feeling we will all have together – a wonderful holiday feeling.

"I didn't kill no one."

"What did you say, Mrs. Salomon?"

"I didn't kill no one."

"Who said that to you?"

"You was taught that. You was taught that and don't tell me different."

"I don't understand. I wasn't taught anything like that."

Mrs. Salomon alternately laughed and cried, her arms hugging her knees. "I never killed nobody," she whimpered. "I'm an old lady."

"Christmas is for all ages."

"It's not my holiday." Standing up she looked directly at Miss Cifano. "It's not my holiday," she shouted. "You did this to point at me. I know what is behind all this. I could tell. I watched what was going on behind my back. Christmas, you kept talking, and there it was – to show me, to
8 make the other patients hate me. I'm not going to come and what will you do when you can't laugh at me? I won't be there. What will you do, Nurse?"

"I won't do anything, Mrs. Salomon. I will be very sorry that you have misunderstood. I am not laughing at you. This is not a religious evening in that sense at all. You have it all wrong."

° ° °

The week preceding Christmas Eve Miss Cifano remained at the hospital every evening after work to supervise the final decorating. Patients assisted her in taping wreaths,

8. It is true, of course, that Christmas *is* a Christian holiday, but it is also important to recognize the way in which this fact is incorporated into Mrs. Salomon's psychopathology. That is, Christmas certainly does have a religious basis, and it is a fact that Mrs. Salomon does not celebrate this holiday. But her interpretation of the Christmas less party as an opportunity to persecute her moves far beyond the initial fact and reflects her psychopathology. Many such delusions have kernels of fact, and it is not always easy to distinguish between fact and pathological fancy.

Santa Claus figures, candy canes and patient drawings on the walls. Miniature Christmas trees were placed on each dining room table. The patient lounge was elaborately decorated with silver and red bells, red and green curtains, and a large Christmas tree festooned with ornaments.

The last job that remained was wrapping gifts for the patient. Each patient was to receive an appropriate gift, one of the many contributed to the hospital. Miss Cifano turned to this activity on December 20th. Miss Young, Miss Rivlen, and several patients volunteered to help. The cartons containing these articles had been stored in the basement, and the attendant was asked to help bring them up to the floor. Permission had been given to use the occupational therapy room to wrap the gifts and to store them until Christmas Eve. The attendant took a floor cart and returned with a number of boxes. Miss Cifano asked him to get the others.

"There aren't any more," he told her.

"There must be," she insisted.

"That all there was. I checked."

Miss Cifano raced downstairs and the woman in charge of the supply room told her someone had been down earlier in the week and taken some boxes.

"But they belonged to me."

"Honey," she said, "whoever come said she was from the fifth floor and she had permission."

"Who was it?"

"Now don't ask me no questions like that. I don't remember."

"But you knew her, otherwise you wouldn't have given her the boxes."

"I forget."

"You *can't* forget. Those were my things. They were for the Christmas party."

"You know I got to keep charge of this room. I got to keep account of all the supplies. I can't stand guard over those boxes. I had to jump around them as it is. You know

I got work to do down here. Whoever came told me they got a right to look at those boxes. How was I supposed to know what she told wasn't the truth?"

With the help of Miss Rivlen and Miss Young, Miss Cifano checked off her inventory. Missing items included large amounts of winter clothing suitable for women, men's sweaters, games such as checkers and chess, playing cards, bottles of cologne and perfume. Miss Cifano was infuriated.

"To have stolen these things was a deliberately malicious act. It is horrible. They were for the patients." She sat on the floor, surrounded by the cartons of articles that still remained. The wrapping paper and ribbons she had bought with her own money were on the floor next to her. Miss Cifano burst into tears.

"They don't need presents. That was overdoing it anyhow," Miss Rivlen said.

"But that isn't the point. Those things belonged to me. They were presents for the patients to be put under the tree. Mr. Reder even promised to play Santa Claus and pass around the gifts." Miss Cifano explained tearfully.

"There's still a lot of stuff," Miss Young reassured her. "Just give each man one of these cigars. It's the idea. They won't notice what they get. Here, you have a box of handkerchiefs. Give each woman one. You didn't promise anyone they would be getting a fancy present, did you?"

Miss Cifano questioned patients and staff about the missing items. No one appeared to know anything about them. The woman in charge of the supply room became angry and went to the administration complaining that she was suspected of being a thief. "After twenty years here no one is going to call me a thief. I have enough to do watching the linens, checking out supplies. Those boxes were put in here and I couldn't stand guard."

Mrs. Burney was informed and she told Miss Cifano that she could not tolerate any more trouble because of the Christmas party. Too many people were becoming upset. She told Miss Cifano that either she must stop asking people about those items or the entire party would have to be called off. Morale was being seriously affected.

* * *

Christmas Eve, Miss Cifano and a few attendants supervised the Christmas party. Mr. Reder, dressed as Santa Claus, handed out gifts. The patients sang songs and ate the food that Miss Cifano and the attendants served. A group of patients made a sincere effort to put on a short skit based on a Christmas theme, but after a few minutes they became enbarrassed and refused to continue.

At nine p.m., interest was flagging and the television set was turned on. The patients lined up their chairs and sat down to watch the program. Except for the voices on television there was complete silence in the room. The floor was littered with cookie crumbs, candy wrappers, paper ribbons, and Christmas wrapping paper. At nine-thirty, Mr. Reder, the attendant, came over to Miss Cifano and told her to leave. "They're all quiet. We got enough people to cover. You go on home. Don't you worry about the floor. We'll take care of it tomorrow."

"It made a difference, didn't it?" asked Miss Cifano. "Don't you think they had fun? It was special, wasn't it?"

"You go on home and have a good time," said Mr. Reder. "Don't you come in tomorrow. I'll be here. I don't have nothing special on tomorrow. We got plenty of help."

Still dressed in costume, Mr. Reder accompanied her to the front door of the hospital. After they had said goodnight and wished each other a happy holiday, Miss Cifano turned to him and said, "Mr. Reder, even if no one said thank you, they really liked the party, didn't they?"

THE CHRISTMAS PARTY

1. Dr. Tanner's address to the staff is concerned with the psychological effects of holidays. He suggests that these periods may induce stress and personal crises. Do you agree with his statements? Have you observed any instances where this happened?

2. Miss Rivlen feels that her patients are unaware of holidays. What might be the basis for her statements? To what extent do you feel her attitude might be a reflection of her own feelings?

3. Miss Cifano agrees with Dr. Tanner and feels that Christmas, in particular, is the one holiday which is particularly upsetting to patients. What evidence does she present to support her observation about patients' depression and stress during the Christmas season?

4. To what extent is Miss Cifano projecting her feelings onto others? Her strong sentiments evoke negative and critical reactions from other staff members. Have you ever been involved in a situation about which you felt strongly only to have other people's perspectives very much at variance with yours? How did their comments and reactions affect you?

5. Miss Cifano enthusiastically outlines a plan to celebrate Christmas to Mrs. Burney, the nursing supervisor. Mrs. Burney tempers Miss Cifano's enthusiasm by pointing out objectives and problems which may arise. How do you feel about Mrs. Burney's appraisal of the difficulties? Would you have preferred her to be carried away by Miss Cifano's plans and to face the problems later? What effects might Mrs. Burney's objectivity have on Miss Cifano?"

6. Think of other situations where you initiated some plan only to have your immediate superiors coolly calculate the pros and cons of carrying out your project. How did

you feel? Did you alter your plans? What alternative ways or approaches would you suggest if you were in Mrs. Burney's position and Miss Cifano came to you for support and assistance?

7. Miss Cifano assumes leadership and secures various levels of cooperation from the staff. What conflicts arise between the preparation of Christmas plans and the carrying out of routine duties? Were any of these clashes avoidable?

8. Can you analyze the dynamics underlying the conflict which develops between Miss Cifano and Mr. Halberstrom? Why might he resist involvement in the project? What are your feelings about his attitude? Why might he be justified in reacting the way he does?

9. Miss Cifano makes every effort to include other people in planning. What patient resentments develop? How do these resentments reflect different perspectives of the same situation? Miss Cifano is convinced of the value of her project and energetically moves towards accomplishing a goal. From her point of view, this goal is a worthwhile and meaningful one. What is your reaction? What were the reactions of other people? Were they justified?

8

"I Didn't Do Anything"

At five-thirty in the morning Timothy Angelo approached the nurse's station, a partitioned enclosure at one end of the corridor. He rapped lightly on the window. Miss Adar, the nurse in charge of the floor, was seated at a center desk completing reports. She glanced up, nodded, motioned for him to wait, and returned to writing. Timothy's tapping became insistent. Each finger singly struck the glass in a steady rhythm.

It was the fifth time during the night that Mr. Angelo had demanded attention. He had been admitted the previous day and had spent a restless night, sleeping for short intervals before awakening and complaining angrily at being locked up in a place where he didn't belong. Sedatives had had no apparent effect on his behavior.

Miss Adar told Miss Warring, an aide, to ask Mr. Angelo to stop hitting the glass. "There are two cracks already, and I'm in no mood for a third at five-thirty in the morning. Not after a night like I've had." Besides Mr. Angelo, Miss Adar had had to give attention to several other extremely restless patients. The ward was short-staffed because two attendants and a nurse had called in sick. Miss Warring went out to Mr. Angelo to relay Miss Adar's message. Timothy's hand was raised, about to strike the window.

He turned abruptly when she came near him, with his arm still raised. Miss Warring stepped back, afraid he was going to hit her. She rushed back to the nurse's station, saying to Miss Adar, "Mr. Angelo is violent and should be seen immediately!"

Miss Adar put her pen down and stood up; at that moment Mr. Angelo pushed the glass and the window splintered. She hurried around the divider of the nurse's area towards Mr. Angelo.

"Don't touch me," he shouted. "I don't belong here. I've been trying to tell you all night. I want out."

"We will talk about that later," said Miss Adar. "I think we better have a look at your hand."

"I want out." Mr. Angelo lifted his arm.

"No, Mr. Angelo. You're going to let me look at your hand. You're going to be calm now. Put your arm down." She reached for his wrist.

"I said, don't touch me!"

Miss Adar tried to explain that she didn't want to touch him against his will, but his hand was bleeding and had to be treated.

"I don't see how I can help you unless you let me look at your hand."

"Can't you see if I hold it up?"

"I can try, but you will have to come closer. I can't very well see from ten feet away. Don't be unreasonable, Mr. Angelo. I'm here to help you. There might be some glass, and I have to get that hand washed. You can see yourself that you're bleeding."

"Not very much," replied Mr. Angelo.

"It's not how much, Mr. Angelo. I just told you there might be some particles of glass." She stepped forward and Mr. Angelo backed away.

"Don't touch me."

"Mr. Angelo, let's be sensible. You've hurt yourself. Are you worried because you broke the glass? No one is going to blame you. Now let's simmer down. The window is broken; you have a cut hand. We have to take care of that first. No one is going to do anything to you without telling you first."

Mr. Angelo was adamant about not wanting Miss Adar to touch any part of his body. He asked if he could have an antiseptic and a Band Aid. He was capable of taking care of it himself. "It's not the first cut I've had in my life. I know what to do about cuts."

"And the glass? You'll need me to take out any glass fragments."

"You don't know if there's glass."

"That's true, but I have to find out."

"How could *you* know? You're not a doctor."

"I'm not the doctor, Mr. Angelo, but I *am* the nurse in charge of the floor. It is my responsibility to take care of you. If necessary, I will call a doctor."

"How do you mean necessary? I got a right to have a doctor. You can't let me bleed to death. You'd get into
(1) trouble. Glass floating around in your stomach can kill you."

"No one is going to let you bleed to death and the glass *won't* go floating in your body. Let me check your hand. I told you I will decide what to do after I look at your hand and get you cleaned up."

"Then will you call a doctor?"

"That might not be necessary."

"I want a doctor now. I have a right to ask for a doctor."

"I am telling you, Mr. Angelo, we will decide that after I examine your hand."

"Like hell you will." Timothy Angelo gripped his injured

1. Note that the nurses statement about the possibility of glass in the cut has now been interpreted by the patient to mean that glass is floating in his stomach. At this point, one can only wonder if this is a temporary reaction to the shock of the accident or if it reflects a more pervasive cognitive disturbance.

hand and leaned against the wall. "Don't come any closer. I stay put. You call a doctor."

Miss Adar returned to the desk and telephoned for a doctor to come to the fifth floor to check a patient's self-inflicted injury. She was told that no one was available but a call was being sent out and someone would come as soon as possible. Miss Adar told Mr. Angelo that a doctor had been requested and he would have to wait until one arrived.

"This wouldn't have happened if I hadn't been stuck here in the first place. It was a big mistake. The doctor said I was going to the hospital to get treated for my neck. He was lying to me. He sent me to a quack who put me here because of some pay-off. There's nothing wrong with me except my neck gets stiff sometimes." He asked Miss Adar if she had called for a *real* doctor or was she trying to pull (2)
a trick on him.

"As soon as I see a real doctor," he told Miss Adar, "he'll know right off that I don't belong here."

Miss Adar went back to complete her records and asked Miss Warring to stand in the hall with Mr. Angelo. She refused, admitting that she was afraid. She told Miss Adar they should call the office and get a security guard.

"We better get the glass cleaned up before someone gets cut."

Miss Warring said she would clean up the nurse's station, and Miss Adar took a broom and dustpan, went into the hall, and began sweeping up the glass. When a doctor

2. The patient refuses to allow the nurse to touch him; he repeatedly says he has been hospitalized by mistake; and he is afraid the nurse will trick him by not calling for a real doctor. Although there may be rational reasons underlying these suspicions, it is also possible that they may reflect an underlying paranoid process. Any diagnostic decision, however, must depend upon further information.

arrived, Miss Adar was emptying the last pieces of glass into a wastebasket.

"What happened?" asked Dr. Sanford.

"The patient broke the glass with his hand."

"Let me see. Kind of early in the morning, isn't it, to go around breaking glass?" he asked Mr. Angelo. "I guess if you're going to break glass, it doesn't matter what time you do it. Didn't anyone clean this up? We'll have to clean it before I can see what's wrong. Why didn't you wash him up?" he asked Miss Adar.

"He wouldn't let me," she replied.

"What do you mean, he wouldn't let you? How long ago did this happen?

"About twenty minutes."

"And you just let him stand here? It seems to me that when there is a choice of cleaning the floor or a bleeding hand, it makes good sense to treat the patient and let the glass stay on the floor. Patients come first. Mavbe that's just my hang-up." He took Mr. Angelo's elbow and escorted him down the hall. "We'll get this cleaned up. Doesn't look too bad. It does seem early in the morning to go breaking windows," he told Mr. Angelo.

After treating Timothy, Dr. Sanford sent him back to his room and returned to the nurses' station for Mr. Angelo's records. While making a notation regarding the accident, he asked Miss Adar why she had neglected to give first aid.

"If you had washed the cuts you would have seen they were only surface scratches and you could have reassured the poor kid. He had some idea he was going to bleed to death. He was shaking with fear."

"He wouldn't let me touch him," explained Miss Adar.

(3) "Not touch him? All you had to do was take his hand. I didn't even ask him. When we got to the sink, he put out

3. In evaluating the situation, Dr. Sanford neglects the possibility that patients may respond quite differently to his hand and that was it. He even kept asking me if he was holding it in the right position." Dr. Sanford emphasized the fact that throughout the examination Mr. Angelo had been docile and cooperative.

"That wasn't the case here. He threatened us every time we took one step closer than ten feet."

"Mr. Angelo?" said Dr. Sanford with surprise. "He's a frightened kid. You misread him completely. He was crying by the time we finished. I asked him if it hurt. He told me no. He was crying because he was scared. By the way," said Dr. Sanford, "it's not such a good idea to tell a patient that he might die from blood poisoning because of glass particles floating in his body."

"I never said anything like that."

Dr. Sanford said that Timothy had reported a conversation with Miss Adar in which she had suggested the threat of poisoning or bleeding to death if his wounds went untreated. Dr. Sanford suggested that Timothy may have exaggerated Miss Adar's remarks, but the general idea was the same. The story had appeared wild to him, but Timothy (4)
insisted that he had been warned about the dangers of bleeding to death by the nurse.

"Anyway, I suppose it's too early in the morning to get the facts straight," said Dr. Sanford. "You better call down and get the window fixed. Have one of the doctors look at

different members of the staff. One commonly assumes that people generally respond to others in about the same way, but in fact there may be a great difference in a patient's behavior as a function of the person with whom he is interacting. An appreciation of the wide range of these differences is important in reconciling behavior reported from different points of view.

4. The patient's initial distortion has become even further magnified.

the hand later today. He's pretty concerned, and it will make him feel better if a doctor checks it."

Miss Warring walked to the elevator with Doctor Sanford. She told him, "Timothy Angelo is really something!" They had had nothing but trouble from him the entire night. She described how he had worried both Miss Adar and herself, and how, after he broke the window, even Miss Adar had been too scared to go out to calm him.

"His hand was coming right at my face. Patients like that should be restrained. Sometimes talking does no good," she insisted. "Miss Adar is usually pretty good, but this one had her coming and going. We sure were glad to see you!"

* * *

Until the previous month, Timothy Angelo had been a first-year student at a small, residential, coeducational college. It was his first experience away from home. Before leaving for school he had lived with his parents and a slightly retarded sister in a small suburban community. His father owned and operated a service station and garage where Timothy worked after school, on weekends, and during summer vacations. His mother kept house and cared for the daughter, whose school attendance was irregular. When Timothy left for college, the mother went to work as a checker in a supermarket across the street from the garage. Since she only worked part-time she was able to look after the house and her daughter when the latter remained at home.

Timothy had attended parochial schools from first grade through high school. Although not an outstanding student, his work was satisfactory, and in his senior year his performance in science and mathematics was above average. On the recommendation of the school guidance counselor, Timothy chose to go away to college rather than attend a school within commuting distance. Mr. Angelo was not eager for Timothy to leave. He needed his son's help in the garage, and Timothy's leaving meant that he would have to hire an assistant during peak hours. Mrs. Angelo, however, was anxious for her son to go away to school. She felt that her earnings could support him. Timothy would (5) be able to work during summers and vacations and assist the family with his educational expenses.

Timothy's first semester was moderately successful. He passed all subjects and received an above average grade in biological sciences. But a few weeks after he returned to the campus to begin the second term, he awakened with a sensation of stiffness in his back. Unable to rise, he stayed in bed until late afternoon when his roommates returned and helped him walk over to the college health service. Timothy was examined; nothing was found, and he was sent to his room to rest. The physician told him to return if he didn't feel better the next day.

The following day Timothy attended classes. At the end of that week, the pains centered in different parts of his body. According to Timothy, "They jump around." At times, his mouth would twitch; then the twitching disappeared and a sensation of "clawing" settled in one foot. Timothy returned to the health service convinced that he had a mysterious disease. A second examination revealed nothing (6) wrong.

At the end of the third week his neck became rigid and

5. The patient's mother is strongly motivated to support her son's education. This might entail considerable pressure on the son to succeed, and he may experience stress in the situation, particularly if his academic abilities are modest in relation to the demands made upon him in college. In working with the patient, it would be important to explore this possibility.

6. The negative findings of the physical examination plus the changing locus of the patient's complaint suggest a psychosomatic basis for the stiffness.

he could not turn it in any position. He said it felt as if an iron bar was running up and down his back, keeping him from moving his head. He telephoned his parents, who told him to come home and see their family doctor.

Shortly after returning home Timothy was checked by the family doctor. His neck was placed in a heat collar, but this did not alleviate the pain and discomfort. No new symptoms developed, but the neck rigidity did not get any better after two weeks of rest at home.

Finally the family physician recommended that Timothy be seen by a psychiatrist. He went to the psychiatrist three times, but then refused to make any more appointments. He insisted it wasn't his mind that was a problem but his neck. "Talking isn't going to solve a neck problem," he said. He felt he must need some kind of drug to cure him.

Timothy's head remained turned to the right at an awkward angle. He could not walk because he could not look forward. His mother had to feed him, and he would stay seated in an armchair all day. At this point, the family doctor and a consulting psychiatrist intervened and Timothy was admitted to the hospital. He was told that he couldn't
(7) be treated at home and hospitalization was necessary in order to diagnose his condition adequately.

* * *

"It's all one big mistake," Timothy told Miss Covington, a nurse who came on duty in the morning.

"What is a mistake, Mr. Angelo?"

7. In trying to understand the possible psychological basis of Mr. Angelo's stiff neck, it is important to note the consequences of this symptom. Specifically, he must return home from college and his mother must care for him almost as though he were a baby. Consequences don't cause a psychological symptom, but they can serve to reinforce or not reinforce a particular behavior.

"My being here. You check the records and you'll see."

"I will look at them later this morning."

"You'll see. Since when do they send a guy with a stiff neck to a mental hospital?"

"I don't think there are mistakes like that. We're here to help you."

"I've been here one day and no one has done anything."

"It takes more than one day."

"Don't they have to take tests and give me some kind of drug? That's all I need – some kind of drug. I read a lot about this. They got drugs, and all I need is some kind of drug so I can move my neck. It must be a special kind of disease." 8

"You *have* been taking medicine."

"Don't kid me. The nurse even told me last night when I couldn't sleep that all she was giving me was a pill to help me sleep. She never said anything about that pill helping my neck."

"You'll be seen."

"When?"

"I'll check. You'll be told."

"So while I wait, I sit around here and suffer."

"Are you in pain now?"

"What do you think? Look at my head. See, it's on the right. I can't turn. It's stiff. To turn it, I have to take my hands and pull it around. The pain kills me." Timothy demonstrated what he had to do to turn his head. He gripped the sides of his face with each hand and wrenched his head to a forward position. When he released his hands his head jerked back to a right angle. "If I don't hold it in place," he told Miss Covington, "that's what it does."

8. A patient may reject a psychological explanation of a physical symptom because it implies personal responsibility for that symptom. In the case of Mr. Angelo, it seems unlikely that he is consciously malingering, and if his stiff neck is indeed psychologically caused, he is probably unaware of it.

Miss Covington told him the doctors would see him later. She suggested that in the meantime he might want to sit down and talk with her.

"What good is talking? My jaw feels stiff. You don't feel like talking with this kind of condition."

Miss Covington suggested that perhaps the two of them could go into the dayroom and play a game of checkers.

"How can I play? I can't look forward."

"We'll put the checker board on the side."

"I don't need checkers," said Timothy. "This is getting me down. I should be back at school. I'm wasting my time here. Can't they just give me a drug and cure this neck? You know, I could die if they don't do anything."

"Now, Mr. Angelo, that's simply not true."

"Yeah?"

"Did anyone tell you that?"

"Sure. How else do you think I got the idea? Some lady last night, not the nurse but one of the attendants, came out and told me I better go back to bed. If I didn't go back to bed, she said, I could die with a condition like this. It could
(9) lead to meningitis. Boy, I felt like batting her one. I bet she goes around scaring people. Now you tell me I can't die, but I don't like that stuff she handed out."

"You're not going to die because of a stiff neck. Now put that notion out of your head. Perhaps you misunderstood what she said."

"It's my neck, not my hearing. I heard OK – you can be sure of that," he said with great assurance.

After he finished talking, his head wobbled back and forth, turned to the right, then snapped sharply over and remained facing left.

"See what just happened?" he asked her.

"No."

9. Once again, Mr. Angelo appears to be either exaggerating or distorting the reactions of others to him.

"My head."

"You tell me what happened, Mr. Angelo."

"Can't you see for yourself? Are you blind or something? It went to the left while I was talking to you. It does that sometimes. I'll be sitting or walking around and then it snaps to the left. It's driving me crazy. It must be a virus (10) that's skipping around like. I once had a virus and they gave me penicillin. I had stiff legs. Why don't they even try a drug on me? They just let me suffer like this. It's getting swollen." His hand stroked his taut neck muscles. "These are new," he added, startled. "I feel some bumps."

Miss Covington put out her hand. Timothy warned her not to come any closer. "Don't touch me. I'll tell you what they are. They're knobs, stiff knobs like they were ready to pop. The attendant last night thought it was all a big joke. It's not funny to me. Maybe she's got some warped sense of humor."

He turned and walked down the corridor using one hand to guide him along the wall.

Miss Covington put out her hand. Timothy warned her Mrs. Dorchester, about Timothy Angelo's nervousness and discomfort. She said that it was a pity that someone had tried to control his behavior through threats rather than through support.

"He told me one of the attendants last night scared him to death."

"Who?"

"He didn't know her name. He said he was up asking for help and an attendant told him he could die from meningitis and a stiff neck."

Mrs. Dorchester was annoyed and expressed her strong disapproval of threats as a means of disciplining patients.

10. The shift, from time to time, in the direction Mr. Angelo must hold his head lends further credence to a psychogenic interpretation of the etiology of his stiff neck.

11 "I have stressed this before at staff meetings," she said. "I guess I'll just have to bring it up again and again."

* * *

Timothy Angelo entered the patient lounge and sat down on the couch next to another patient. He held his head in both hands and moaned. Mr. Farber, the other patient, asked him what was wrong, and Timothy said he had a virus and his neck was stiff. "But I don't think I'm contagious," he added.

Mr. Farber became worried and said that Timothy must tell a nurse at once. Timothy replied that he had been trying to do that ever since he had arrived but without any success. "Everyone around here runs away when you try and tell them your problems."

He described how he had just talked to Miss Covington, a nurse in the hall, and told her about his pain, and her reply was that his imagination was playing tricks. Mr. Angelo said he knew that some illnesses were psychosomatic, but his doctor as well as the doctor at the hospital had told him that he had a virus and that they were leaving orders with a nurse to give him hourly medicine. "The nurse knew this," explained Timothy, "and she wanted me to play checkers!" He shrugged his shoulders. "I guess nothing can be done when you're locked up."

"That's not true," replied Mr. Farber, a man in his early sixties. "Patients have legal rights." He told Timothy to telephone his family. In the meantime, he would locate Mr. Beecher, an attendant who could be relied upon in emergencies.

"Sometimes you got to use pull around here. The nurses run out like this and make up stories. They don't want to

11. Note that, without checking, Mrs. Dorchester appears to accept as valid the reported use of threat. Thus a rumor continues to be circulated.

take the time to get the medicine." Very upset, Mr. Farber told Mr. Angelo to stay put while he went out to get help.

Mr. Beecher, who had been an attendant on the male ward for ten years, came in to talk to Timothy. Timothy rubbed his neck and complained of its stiffness. He also told Mr. Beecher that his hand was throbbing.

"Some doctor tried to fix it last night but he said he couldn't stitch it up because it would take time and he was supposed to be off duty anyhow."

"How did it happen?" asked Mr. Beecher.

"I couldn't sleep," answered Timothy. "I went out to call a nurse. A nurse came out and started to push me. I guess she was mad because it was early in the morning and she didn't want to be bothered. I don't like to be any trouble, but I also don't like the idea of being pushed around. I couldn't hit her. I sort of pretended to lift my hand and then she grabbed me and my hand went back and hit the glass."

"I saw the broken window," said Mr. Beecher. "We wondered what went on here last night."

"Now you know. She told me I was nothing but trouble around here and all that happened was that I couldn't get to sleep. I just came here yesterday. She finally sent for a doctor. I knew she had to. She accused me of trying to fake out. I couldn't sleep, I told her. That knocked her. I guess you learn pretty fast not to ask for some help to make you sleep."

"Don't feel that way," said Mr. Beecher reassuringly. "Maybe she had had a hard night. Did she tell you to wait or anything?"

"She didn't say anything. First she sent out some other character who ran back and said I was the violent type."

"You don't look violent," said Mr. Beecher. "That bandage is pretty dirty. I'll get a nurse to change it."

"No, the doctor told me not to touch it until this afternoon. He said he wanted a doctor to look at it."

"I think Dr. Eckhardt is up on the floor," said Mr. Beecher. "I'll check."

Mr. Beecher located Dr. Eckhardt at the elevator and asked him if he would mind taking a few extra minutes to change a patient's bandage. He said that the patient had had a very difficult night and was very worried. Evidently he had been frightened by what he had perceived as an attack by a nurse. Mr. Beecher described him as a quiet, serious young boy who seemed in pain and was trying to put on a brave front.

Dr. Eckhardt went in to see Timothy.

"I understand you had a bad night," commented Dr. Eckhardt.

"I don't want to talk about it," said Timothy.

"Perhaps we should try. Is there anything wrong?"

"Yeah, maybe there is," said Timothy slowy. "I kind of wonder what made that nurse on duty try to scare me. It bothers me."

"What did she say?"

"She said that I could bleed to death from a wound like this. Of course I know better. But she got me worked up telling me that the glass could kill me if it got into my bloodstream. You know, when they scare you like that and you're kind of half awake it does things to you."

"I agree," said Dr. Eckhardt. "It wasn't the wisest thing to have said."

"I'm glad to hear you say that."

"Who was it?"

"The nurse last night."

"Do you remember her name?"

"No, I wouldn't want to get her into any kind of trouble. She was the only nurse out there. It was about five-thirty in the morning."

"What did she do?"

"She finally called a doctor."

"Did he come?"

"After a couple of hours," said Timothy. "I don't blame

him. He said his coming was a waste of time. The nurse should have cleaned the cut. Then he washed my hand, which the nurse should have done, and told me that maybe I needed stitches because of the way the gash cut through the skin. See, right here at the thumb. He wanted to go off duty. I can't blame him after working all night. He looked pretty bad. I told him to forget it and he said he could clean it out and then today another doctor would do the sewing. How many stitches will it need, Doctor?" (12)

"None," replied Dr. Eckhardt. "What did you say the name of the doctor was?"

"I didn't," answered Timothy. "I don't like to get him in trouble. He was a kind of young guy, had a small beard and glasses – about my height and his hair was dark brown, almost black. I think he said something about being the only one on duty last night. Just forget it, will you Doctor? I appreciate what you've done. Should I get the bandage changed again today?"

* * *

Timothy telephoned his mother and told her that he had been hurt and she had better come immediately to the hospital. Within an hour she appeared and after assuring herself that Timothy's injuries were not serious, she asked to see Mrs. Dorchester. She told her she was upset at her son's story of receiving brutal treatment from a nurse his first night at the hospital, and about how a second nurse had neglected to give him medicine for his severe neck (13)

12. Once again, Mr. Angelo's report of his experiences is distorted and exaggerated; however, one cannot infer from this that he is consciously lying. He may indeed be unable to distinguish between truth and fantasy. But perhaps it is more important to recognize in this case the effect Mr. Angelo's distortions have on other people.

13. Note that Mr. Angelo's experience is now reported as an instance of brutal treatment.

pains. Mrs. Dorchester said she couldn't understand the nurses behaving in such a way.

"You weren't there," said Mrs. Angelo. "My son does not tell stories. He is a very truthful young man. I have never had the usual problems of most parents. I think that was the way my husband and I brought him up. His school wouldn't stand for any nonsense. Do you know, they wanted him to consider a religious life? He's always been outstanding in science. I hope some day he will study medicine. I think he wants to be a doctor. I don't understand why he was treated this way. I could understand if he was one of those hippy kind of boys. But he isn't. He's very neat. He has short hair. He never let his hair grow. You can see yourself what a fine looking boy he is."

"The length of hair doesn't make a difference in the way we treat our patients, Mrs. Angelo."

"Are you sure?"

"Of course, I'm sure."

"Were you here last night or today with the other nurse?"

"No."

"Then you can't know what happened. My son was the one who was pushed around."

"Our nurses don't push patients around."

"Just a little bit if they get angry?" asked Mrs. Angelo.

"Not at all."

"They never get angry?"

"I didn't say that," replied Mrs. Dorchester.

"That proves it," said Mrs. Angelo. "They got angry at my son."

"I will look into the matter," said Mrs. Dorchester.

"I hope you do," said Mrs. Angelo. "I'd hate going home knowing my son and other poor patients who couldn't do anything are being pushed around in a hospital when they're supposed to be getting helped."

On her way out, Mrs. Angelo noticed Dr. Eckhardt and asked if she might speak to him a moment about a problem. She reported that she was the mother of a patient who was struck by a nurse and had to have his hand stitched. She wondered if Dr. Eckhardt knew her son. He said that he had looked at her son's hand and that no stiches were required.

"It doesn't matter if there are stitches or not," said Mrs. Angelo. "What bothers me is the way the people around here threatened him. He probably didn't tell you. He's not the kind of boy who likes to tell stories and get people in trouble, but he told me that the people around here called him awful names. One said he was crazy. I don't think that it is right. You can imagine what that did to him. I know he's all in a knot and upset. Believe me, I know. He wouldn't be here otherwise. But what is gained by telling him that he is crazy? I know everyone here works hard and gets tired. But you can't tell a patient he's crazy."

Dr. Eckhardt apologized for any misunderstanding. He said that he didn't like to believe that the staff criticized the patients.

"Well, in my son's case they did."

Observing their discussion, Mrs. Dorchester came over and Dr. Eckhardt briefly told her that Mrs. Angelo was disturbed at the treatment accorded her son. They both assured Mrs. Angelo that the matter would be investigated and taken care of.

"I hope so," said Mrs. Angelo.

After she left, Dr. Eckhardt talked to Mrs. Dorchester about the problem and emphasized the need for discretion in speaking to patients.

"My staff does not call people crazy."

"I am not saying that anyone did that," said Dr. Eckhardt. "But they should be reminded that patients might react to any hint of an insult. We shouldn't forget this."

"But I know no staff member would call any patient crazy."

"That isn't the point. It's a matter of being in control. You know, you can say one thing, but your tone of voice will communicate something else. This might very well be what happened. It's not only the nursing staff, but I will have to look into what happened with Dr. Sanford. I know he had a rough night. Evidently Timothy Angelo got the brunt of his fatigue. This happens to all of us, but that is not an excuse for rudeness."

The administrative office telephoned Mrs. Dorchester later that afternoon to report that Mrs. Angelo, a patient's mother, had registered a complaint about staff mistreatment of her son. She said that there were patient witnesses to the verbal abuse. Mrs. Dorchester said that she could not affirm or deny the charges but that she was looking into the matter. The secretary in the office said that Mrs. Angelo had threatened to bring a lawsuit against the hospital for physical violence that had created nervous tension in her son.

Dr. Eckhardt was informed of Mrs. Angelo's complaint and he suggested to Mrs. Dorchester that she make inquiries and try to discover exactly what had happened. He also spoke to Dr. Sanford, telling him that since Timothy's hand had not required stiches he wondered why Dr. Sanford had suggested this as a possibility to him.

Dr. Sanford denied having said anything about stitches. On the contrary, he had wondered why an emergency call had been placed at all. The cuts were superficial scratches. The nurse in charge had not taken the trouble to look at the hand, and the patient had been extremely tense by the time he arrived.

Dr. Eckhardt thought the tension might have been a result of Timothy's waiting several hours in a state of anxiety. Dr. Sanford replied that he had come the moment he was free and insisted that the delay could not have been more than thirty minutes.

Their conversation was interrupted; however, Dr. Sanford was left with the feeling that his superior, Dr. Eckhardt, did not entirely believe what he had said. He was troubled by Dr. Eckhardt's final remark: "We all reach a point of fatigue. It comes out sometimes in what we say without our being aware of the implications."

The next day, when Dr. Sanford spoke to Mrs. Dorchester,

he implied that the nursing staff was failing to meet its responsibilities to the patients. "Matters which a nurse should take care of are being referred to doctors." He cited the example of Timothy Angelo, who was led to believe that his
wounds were serious because the nurse had not taken the 14
trouble to look, but chose to refer a simple cut to a doctor.

Mrs. Dorchester did not answer the criticism of her staff directly, but said that the wards were understaffed, and on that evening three staff people were absent. This had placed a burden on one nurse, who had had to take full charge of a very large ward with a minimum of assistance.

Mrs. Dorchester spoke individually to a number of the staff, trying to find out what had happened. She felt that the pressure to resolve this incident was mounting. The administrative offices made a second call; Dr. Eckhardt had asked for a follow-up of the case, and Dr. Sanford intimated that the fault could be attributed to laxity on the part of the nursing staff.

She met with several attendants, each of whom reported different versions of the events. Miss Warring, in particular, said that every time anything went wrong around the hospital, the attendants were blamed. She resented this. She was tired of being walked over by the nurses. Mr.
Beecher didn't feel this way, but he did maintain that the 15
staff was inconsistent in its relationships with the attendants.

"Sometimes they will tell you to do something and other times they will tell you that you are an attendant and shouldn't try to do a nurse's job." He felt that he had been around enough to know that there wasn't a job around the hospital he couldn't manage. "Trouble is," he said, "no one appreciates what you do around here. You can work yourself to the bone without any real thanks."

14. A pecking order has been established: Dr. Eckhardt admonishes Dr. Sanford, who in turn admonishes Mrs. Dorchester.

15. Under stress, other problems become apparent.

In talking with the staff nurses, Mrs. Dorchester reviewed the facts, reporting that Timothy felt that the nursing staff was abusive. She spoke about expressing feelings to patients. "It may very well have been that you were tired," she told
16 Miss Adar, "but fatigue certainly isn't any excuse for one's actions or words."

Miss Adar insisted that she had not been curt or derogatory in any way. Mr. Angelo refused to let her take care of his hand and she had no alternative but to phone for a doctor. She didn't know if Mr. Angelo had heard Miss Warring describe him as violent and suggested that this might be what bothered Timothy. She admitted that Dr. Sanford had been annoyed with her.

"He had no right to be. I tried to wash that patient's hand. He absolutely refused to let me near him."

"Dr. Sanford said that he was cooperative. Did you tell Timothy he was going to need stitches?"

"I never said that," retorted Miss Adar.

"He wasn't worried so much about stitches," interrupted Miss Covington, "but he said that he had been told he might
17 die from a stiff neck. I thought that was unfortunate. Someone must have given him that idea."

16. The pecking order continues as Mrs. Dorchester admonishes the nursing staff.

17. Because of the expressed and implied threat in this situation, the people involved have taken a defensive position, assuming the roles of detective and prosecutor in their efforts to discover the true story. Thus, their professional helping roles as doctors, nurses, and attendants have been obscured. No one has thus far focused his attention on trying to understand Mr. Angelo, who may be the source of their current difficulties, but is, after all, the patient in need of their help. If greater attention had been paid to Mr. Angelo, perhaps a fuller understanding of his psychodynamics and

"I didn't say anything to him about that," answered Miss Adar. "I didn't know anything about his stiff neck. He was up five times that first night and his only complaint was that he wanted to leave the hospital, that he wasn't crazy and didn't belong here in the first place."

Miss Adar and Miss Covington debated the different versions of the story. Miss Covington insisted that she wasn't blaming Miss Adar for having upset Timothy, but Timothy had told her that a nurse had been quite angry and said he could die from the virus if it remained untreated.

Miss Adar emphatically denied knowing anything about Timothy's neck. "I hadn't read his records," she said. "He had only been admitted that day, and I didn't know anything about his neck."

Several other staff members said that his stiff neck was obvious. "You only had to look at him and see that he had trouble turning his head," commented one of them.

Miss Adar expressed anger toward the resident, Dr. Sanford, who had come up to the floor and complained about her without listening to her story of what had happened.

"I have known plenty of times," she said, "when patients begged to have any other doctor but him come to look at them."

Mrs. Dorchester suggested that the discussion was getting out of hand. She stressed the need to be careful of what you say and how you say it. "At this point," she admitted, "I'm not sure of who said what to whom."

In the following days, Timothy Angelo complained continually about his treatment by the nursing staff, attendants, and doctors. He insisted that he was being purposefully avoided. He noticed that all of them turned in the other direction when they saw him approaching.

social behavior might have short-circuited some of the difficulties in communication that developed among members of the staff.

"Everyone is after me," he told Mr. Farber. "They're eager enough to take money. But they don't give you anything in return. What kind of help am I getting? If I stay here, I can only get worse. They don't care what happens. Look at the broken window out there. They put tape on the crack. They don't even fix broken windows. Broken windows can be dangerous. Someone could cut himself. And my neck. Who cares if I'm going crazy with this neck? I ask for some drug and they act like I'm poison. What did I do to any of them? I didn't do anything. I am here in the first place because of a fluke. Some doctors don't know what is wrong, so the first thing they do is put you in a mental hospital. I never did a thing to any of them around here, and for all they care, I'm dirt. You can't trust any of them—doctors, nurses, attendants. They lie through their teeth at the drop of a hat!"

"I DIDN'T DO ANYTHING"

1. Timothy Angelo repeatedly requests the nurse's attention. The hour is late; the staff is limited; Miss Adar has pressing responsibilities and shifts the burden of taking care of his latest request to an aide. Was she right? Discuss the problem of delegation of responsibility. Are there any guidelines regarding the functions and responsibilities of different staff personnel in the situation in which you are currently working?

2. After Timothy breaks the glass, he resists the nurse's efforts to take care of his wound. Evaluate Miss Adar's approach to him. Considering his behavior, did she have any alternative but to call for a doctor? In this instance, would you be concerned about your inability to handle the situation?

3. How do you feel about Dr. Sanford's comments about

Miss Adar's supposed neglect in taking care of Timothy? How might Dr. Sanford have checked the validity of Timothy's remarks without threatening Miss Adar?

4. Dr. Sanford discusses the events in Timothy's presence. At times staff members do converse in front of patients. What problems may arise because of this practice? The assumption may be that patients are not paying attention or are unaware of the discussions. Why might the staff assume that patients aren't listening or aware?

5. Miss Warring feels compelled to comment on Timothy's obstructive behavior to Dr. Sanford. Why might she feel the need to stress the fact that Timothy is a very difficult patient?

6. Timothy denies having any psychiatric disturbance, insisting that his condition is completely physical. The denial of mental illness poses a number of problems which may hinder the development of a therapeutic relationship. Can you indicate what these may be?

7. In Timothy's case, what purpose may his denial of mental illness have in terms of his self concept? Do you feel it might be necessary to break through this barrier of denial before establishing a therapeutic relationship?

8. Timothy reports various stories about his treatment to Miss Covington, the content of which troubles her. In presenting the information to the head nurse, what assumption has Miss Covington made regarding the validity of Timothy's statements?

9. In each of his subsequent encounters with staff members, Timothy relates what appear to be rational accounts of events or conversations. How are they accepted by the staff members? Do you feel that Timothy's assertions should have been challenged?

10. Because the staff accepts Timothy's reports as valid,

they behave and react accordingly. What is the chain of reaction each tale sets in motion? Characterize the reactions of each staff member. Discuss the problems involved in trying to decide if a patient's impressions are distortions of fact.

11. Can you give examples of similiar instances where a patient's misinterpretations affected staff attitudes toward each other as well as toward the patient?

12. Timothy craves attention, and yet his every action works against his desire. What can be done to help this kind of patient, whose behavior is self-defeating?